JOY
IN DARK PLACES

JOY
IN DARK PLACES

Thomas Parr

Reformation Heritage Books
Grand Rapids, Michigan

Joy in Dark Places
© 2022 by Thomas Parr

Reformation Heritage Books
3070 29th St. SE
Grand Rapids, MI 49512
616–977–0889
orders@heritagebooks.org
www.heritagebooks.org

Scripture taken from the New King James Version®. Copyright © 1982 by Thomas Nelson. Used by permission. All rights reserved.

Printed in the United States of America
22 23 24 25 26 27/10 9 8 7 6 5 4 3 2 1

Library of Congress Cataloging-in-Publication Data

Names: Parr, Thomas (Thomas M.), author.
Title: Joy in dark places / Thomas Parr.
Description: Grand Rapids, Michigan : Reformation Heritage Books, [2022] | Includes bibliographical references.
Identifiers: LCCN 2022001150 (print) | LCCN 2022001151 (ebook) | ISBN 9781601789266 (paperback) | ISBN 9781601789273 (epub)
Subjects: LCSH: Joy—Religious aspects—Christianity. | Happiness—Religious aspects—Christianity. | Light and darkness in the Bible. | BISAC: RELIGION / Christian Living / Spiritual Warfare
Classification: LCC BV4647.J68 P37 2022 (print) | LCC BV4647.J68 (ebook) | DDC 248.4—dc23/eng/20220210
LC record available at https://lccn.loc.gov/2022001150
LC ebook record available at https://lccn.loc.gov/2022001151

For additional Reformed literature, request a free book list from Reformation Heritage Books at the above regular or email address.

Contents

Introduction

Christians often find themselves to be miserable instead of joyful, and deep down they know something is very wrong. They are aware that their loss of joy is tragic, but they think they can't help it, that in the end it doesn't really matter, and that having a joyful life is an unattainable ideal. This book was written to dispel this hopelessness and to kindle joy despite the multitude of things trying to snuff it out.

Gaining biblical joy means you must resolutely confront yourself: you encounter truth in God's Word and believe it to be true in your case, then you align your emotions with it, despite your circumstances. The psalmist does this when he confronts his depressed self: "Why are you cast down, O my soul? And why are you disquieted within me? Hope in God, for I shall yet praise Him for the help of His countenance" (Ps. 42:5). Martyn Lloyd-Jones commented on this verse, saying, "You have to take yourself in hand, you have to address yourself, preach to yourself.... Remind yourself of God.... Then having done that...defy yourself...and say with this man: 'I shall yet praise Him for the help of His countenance.'"[1] "Defy yourself" isn't an overstatement. The psalmist banishes displeasure at circumstances and embraces God's truth decisively, even aggressively. He urges the reasons for joy on himself, regardless of his hardships. This self-defiance presumes that there is something within us that resists biblical joy and must be confronted (Gal. 5:17).

---

1. David Martyn Lloyd-Jones, *Spiritual Depression* (Grand Rapids: Eerdmans, 1992), 21.

Maintaining joy requires using Scripture in faith persistently. Since you resist joy yourself, you cannot rely on one experience of victory. You have to reassert truth continually. You keep praying in light of it, using its brilliance to dispel your soul's darkness, which always wants to creep back in. Pouring oil in the lamp keeps the room lit, and stocking a stove keeps it warm. Biblical joy is fueled by the Word: "I will delight myself in Your commandments, which I love" (Ps. 119:47). You must keep your soul well-lit and warm with continual and fresh supplies of biblical truth.

Maintaining joy also requires relying on the Spirit. It is hard to confront your wayward emotions and persistently rejoice in truth rather than groan in hardship. It goes against our fallen natures. It is hard to overcome tiredness and put off sin and "every weight" holding you back (Heb. 12:1). All this requires a Spirit-empowered resolve, setting your face like flint to put to death what is earthly in you. You cannot fight the flesh with the flesh, so you must continually make use of the only antidote to the flesh's withering and enfeebling influence, the Spirit of God.

Maintaining joy requires really banking on the good news about a merciful God. You have to really believe that God loves you forever and provides all your needs. Otherwise, the clamor and din of a fallen world will win out in your soul. But the gospel assures Christians that they have peace with God by faith (Rom. 5:1), that all things work for their good (8:28), that mercy will follow them all their days (Ps. 23:6), and that nothing can separate them from God's love (Rom. 8:35). Christians fail to have joy because they haven't fully or consistently grasped the greatness of these things. Their emotions haven't yet learned to harmonize with the gospel's tones. They haven't fully experienced the sweetness of Christ or fully known the height and depth of God's love, at least not enough that their knowledge affects their emotions when in hardship. They don't feel safe in Christ's arms because they haven't yet realized that the gospel is a flood of light for all dark places.

"Dark places" refers to anything that challenges our joy. Some of this book's chapters address things that are truly dark, like the moral evil of legalism or results of the fall such as old age, dying, problem people in the church, and societal disintegration. Other chapters address things often misunderstood as dark, like law and conviction of sin. Every chapter shows how the gospel dispels anxiety over circumstances and brings profound joy instead. Whether we're talking moral evil, calamity, or misunderstanding, the gospel is the answer.

The first two chapters of the book define joy and show some basics for experiencing it. Chapters 3–10 show how the gospel sheds light on dark places people often create when they think about God's commands: they avoid conviction, fearfully wonder if the Bible teaches "works-salvation" after all, subtly rely on their performance, and don't grasp the true freedom the gospel gives. Beginning in chapter 11, each chapter stands alone and sheds gospel light on a discrete topic that often challenges joy. Chapter 17 deals with how we can possibly have joy when we know that the last judgment will be according to our works.

This book primarily addresses Christian thinking and experience. It is about the head and the heart. Applications for us to "do" can be found throughout, but the focus is on whether our inner lives are really in accord with our faith and thus whether our "doing" really flows from that inner life. Are we shedding God's light in our dark places and rejoicing there? The gospel is supposed to produce a "soundtrack of the soul," an inner song that is described as rejoicing (e.g., Ps. 97:12; Hab. 3:18; Rom. 12:12).

When we are cast down and have changed the soundtrack, we need to reassert the biblical reasons to rejoice. As we saw above, David did so in Psalm 42. On another occasion, when all his men turned against him and were about to take his life, "David strengthened himself in the LORD his God" (1 Sam. 30:6). On yet another occasion, when people told him that matters were hopeless and that he should "flee as a bird," he replied that the Lord was on His heavenly throne watching all people (see Ps. 11:1–4). David gained spiritual ballast in truth about God. He grounded his soul in theology and gained joy from it.

But many people don't derive joy from theology. They strengthen themselves in films, games, food, or social connections rather than thoughts of God. These things either are or can be blessings, and we ought to rejoice in good things. But if this book is about anything, it is about instilling a spiritual habit of rejoicing in the primary and best thing—God's salvation in Christ through the Spirit. That is the purpose of every chapter, pointing us to the dazzling light of Christ.

For someone outside of Christ, encountering dark places in life should be a profoundly disturbing experience. Dark things such as temporal judgments, an unclean conscience, and aging are foretastes of doom for unbelievers. For them, every unpleasant thing is just a sample of the Great Unpleasant of the afterlife. But Christians are encouraged to "rejoice in the Lord always" (Phil. 4:4) because they have a basis, even a necessity, for it in Christ. The question is whether we will truly appropriate God's promises by faith and bank on eternal, unseen things. It is my prayer that the gospel will always brighten your life, even—especially—when you are in dark places.

CHAPTER 1

Joy and Its Obstacles

Rejoice always, pray without ceasing, in everything give thanks; for this is the will of God in Christ Jesus for you.
—1 Thessalonians 5:16–18

It is probably not an overstatement to say that a joyless Christian is, or ought to be, a contradiction. Experiencing Christ's salvation is supposed to have a dramatic impact on us and transform our lives into ones of holy delight. But we may not be experiencing biblical joy because we do not understand what it is. People can even be suspicious of joy, as if it were frivolous merriment. Or they might resist the idea that biblical joy is emotional at all. Others may simply not see why joy is important, and still others are among the host of people who allow difficulties to snuff it out.

In this chapter, let's define biblical joy from Scripture and see why it is absolutely crucial. Then we'll consider more closely the problem of dark places that can quench it, even things we may feel come from the Bible itself.

Biblical Joy

Biblical joy is an emotion of gladness. You might be tempted to think of joy as an ideal, an act of the will, or an objective reality rather than an emotional state. I suspect people think of it in these terms because they either don't have emotional joy in God (and feel bad about their lack) or they are suspicious of emotionalism. It is true that emotionalism—minimizing doctrine and the intellect in favor of emotion—is a terrible problem in our times. But it doesn't follow that joy itself is a problem. And if our hearts are dead like stones, we should not distort the verses that point out our deficiency.

Joy is clearly an emotional state of gladness in contrast to sorrow or misery. This definition is not just common sense but is reflected in Scripture. Jesus described joy as the opposite of sorrow when He told the disciples, "Your sorrow will be turned into joy" (John 16:20). Paul contrasted joy with sorrow too (2 Cor. 2:3). This fundamental starting point profoundly affects how we live. If we do not see joy as an emotion that is the opposite of misery, then our Christian life will be very different from someone who sees it as such. One person will ensure that their theology leads them to the emotional state of joy and will not be content otherwise, while the other person might tolerate deadness or even hypocritical externalism, outward show without inward reality.

Biblical joy is empowering. It strengthens you to do right in hardship: "The joy of the LORD is your strength" (Neh. 8:10). Jesus warned us that "in the world you will have tribulation" (John 16:33), but Christians are not to give up, be morose, or be outraged at trials. They are to be so joyful that they have the strength to overcome the crushing weight of hardship. Far from being of marginal importance, the emotion of biblical joy is necessary for spiritual power.

Joy comes from meditating on the Word of God. Jesus prayed, "These things I speak in the world, that they may have My joy fulfilled in themselves" (John 17:13). Jesus says that He spoke His words to produce joy in His disciples; His purpose in giving the Word is to foster it. The prophet Jeremiah testified to experiencing that same joy: "Your words were found, and I ate them, and Your word was to me the joy and rejoicing of my heart" (Jer. 15:16). God does not mean for such an experience to be a momentary sentiment; it is to be an eternal delight: "Your testimonies I have taken as a heritage forever, for they are the rejoicing of my heart" (Ps. 119:111). When Spirit-filled people nourish their souls in the Word, they gain joy. Perhaps we're joyless because we're Word-less. More than ever, our society provides endless opportunities to immerse ourselves in things other than the Bible, so it is entirely possible that the happiness we experience is not Word-centered and thus not biblical joy.

Biblical joy is supposed to be consistent. "Rejoice in the Lord always," Paul taught (Phil. 4:4). God's salvation is boundless, and therefore joy should be too. When we consider what God has done for us in Christ and by faith assert it in dark places, joy results; it is like standing in a dreadful cave and holding aloft a blazing torch. But if we do not meditate on Scripture, we'll just stand in the shadows, letting it creep into our souls. We fail to have joy because circumstances are real to us and biblical doctrine is not. But fixing our gaze on Christ gives joy by the power of the Spirit.

Biblical joy should be normative in comparison to other emotions. It should not often be superseded by other emotions—and never by sinful ones. Joy isn't the only emotion we should experience, and it's a mistake to think that it is. God wants us to abhor evil, be convicted of sin, weep with those who weep, and sorrow over the fate of the wicked. All these emotions are right for us to feel, and sometimes such emotions should even temporarily be prominent in our hearts. After all, Jesus Himself wept when He beheld the effect of His friend's death on his family (John 11:35) and was grieved at people's hard hearts (Mark 3:5). Weeping and grieving are akin to sorrow; sorrow's opposite, joy, cannot take precedence in a heart that is experiencing it. All this leads us to conclude that "rejoice in the Lord always" doesn't mean "be happy all the time, every second." That is a shallow understanding that doesn't grapple with the complexity of living in a fallen world, and it doesn't square with Scripture either. Being around someone who plasters on a smile all the time, thinking they're obeying Philippians 4:4, would be unbearable.

"Rejoice in the Lord always" isn't a simplistic thing. It does mean rejoicing in the Lord consistently, however, and also not allowing other godly emotions to move joy from the normative position. Whatever emotion may temporarily need to take center stage, it shouldn't override joy's primary place. It is crucial to see. There are few things Paul explicitly says to do *always*, but rejoicing in the Lord is one of them.

Joy's prominent role should not displace other normative emotions that are to be reflected in the Christian soul: peace, compassion, and reverence, for example. It is wrong to displace reverence to make room for an unrestrained and excessive joy. This is a problem with much Christian worship in our day. Despite the reality of abuses, joy is supposed to be the norm. Not experiencing it is abnormal and unhealthy. Additionally, many emotions are always sinful and are absolute joy-killers—strife, outbursts of rage, grudges (Gal. 5:19–20). Joy in Christ must never give place to these, for the Spirit must overcome the flesh.

Ask yourself if joy is normative in your life or if you are characterized by some other emotion. Has another emotion, perhaps even a good one, displaced joy? That should not be. Serious-minded Christians could be militant against sin yet be so grim that they are joyless. That's not a good advertisement for Christianity. Worse, it seems a betrayal of the gospel that promotes boundless joy, even in the dark places of a sin-cursed world and a crooked generation.

Biblical joy is Spirit-empowered. "The fruit of the Spirit is…joy" (Gal. 5:22). This is good news to those who are troubled by their own gloomy tendencies. When the Spirit is present, He generates joy. If we do not have joy, we either do not have the Spirit (and are therefore not believers) or we are quenching Him. If we are quenching Him, we must confess our rebellion, seek Christ for the Spirit's filling, and stock our souls with the Spirit's kindling, the Word. The answer to any sin problem is the Word of God in a Spirit-filled heart (Ps. 119:11; Gal. 5:16). If you find it difficult to be joyful and even have fallen into arguing against its necessity, turn now from that unbiblical path and begin cultivating a life of joy. How delightful to know that this life of joy is what God wants for you.

Biblical joy is productive. Sometimes people might misunderstand an emphasis on joy as encouragement of complacency. The people who are in the trenches and working hard do not like the idea of people just sitting joyfully at Jesus's feet (Luke 10:40). Looks like laziness! But biblical joy isn't a way to avoid activity; rather, we should view it as an approach to activity, like a spice that seasons all our actions. "Rejoice before the LORD…in all to which you put your hands" (Deut. 12:18). It must be said that many Christian people ought to be working hard and are not. God's work often languishes while people happily fiddle in their homes (Hag. 1:9). Yes, such people must repent and start serving God, but we do not want them to do so with a grump and a groan. We should never encourage people to serve the Lord unless they are motivated by joy. Perhaps people don't want to serve in the church because they've seen the repelling way we do it. For Christians, joy and activity must go hand in hand.

Biblical joy seeks expression in public worship on the Lord's Day. "This is the day the LORD has made; we will rejoice and be glad in it" (Ps. 118:24). Let me quickly explain two points from this verse and then draw an application. First, the "day" it speaks of is the day of Christ's resurrection. We know this because the context mentions a stone being rejected and then exalted to the head of the corner (v. 22). This is the metaphor for Christ's crucifixion and resurrection that the apostle Peter used (Acts 4:11–12). Second, the day on which Christ rose from the dead was the first day of the week, Sunday, known in Scripture as the Lord's Day (Mark 16:2; Rev. 1:10). Here is the application for believers today: Psalm 118 pictures us rejoicing and being glad on the day of resurrection, or Sunday. In the New Testament we find that believers make this experience permanent—they make it a norm to gather on Sunday to celebrate Christ's Supper and hear His Word (Acts 20:7). We see from this that biblical joy isn't content alone; it must find others who rejoice. The church is the result as believers seek Christ and are glad in Him on the Lord's Day.

Biblical joy is Christ-centered. The joy God wants us to experience is not just happiness in general but rather joy in Christ. The phrase "in the Lord" (Phil. 4:4) means two things: Christ is the subject in which we take joy and the basis for being joyful. Let's look more closely at these two ideas.

Christ is the *subject* in which we take joy. Biblical joy is centered on Christ, not on things that a person who doesn't know Him can experience. Many today have accepted that we should learn to enjoy Christ in nature, sports, or travel, and I would agree that we should do so. But if you find no joy in the revelation of Christ found in the Bible, I wonder about your enjoyment of these other things, and you should too. Christians love Christ (1 Cor. 16:22). They take great delight at thoughts of Him (Mal. 3:16). They keep their eyes fixed on Him (Heb. 12:2). Their heart is with Him in heaven (Col. 3:1–4). We instinctively understand what "I love this person" means when it refers to a friend, but somehow I fear that people can fool themselves into thinking they love God when they demonstrate little interest in Him at all. Ask yourself if you cherish thoughts of Jesus Christ and if you wish to think and speak and hear of Him as much as you can.

Christ provides the *basis for experiencing joy*. The joy that God wants you to have is justifiable because it is rooted in biblical doctrine—God chose us in Christ from eternity, sent Him into the world to live and die for us, and raised Him from the dead to intercede for us always and continue His good work in us till He returns for us. Without these truths there is no basis for having joy in this sin-cursed world full of lies and cruelty and death. But when you see what Christ has done, is doing, and will do, there is reason to rejoice. In fact, choosing gloom belittles Him and says, "My problems outweigh Your salvation," or to put it more theologically, "The misery of the fall is greater than Your redemption."

Joy's Importance

Understanding Christ as the basis for our joy shows why it is so important. Choosing joy asserts that its basis is real—indeed, overwhelming—to all miseries that challenge it. Joy says Christ really is greater than all negatives. Choosing joy in Christ honors God's work of redemption as something so glorious that it ought to impart sweetness to our souls always, no matter how bad things get. The tones of my soul must absolutely be harmonizing with the gospel. Nothing must ever displace Christ or override His salvation— nothing. The soul is like a music center in which a soundtrack always plays, and we must be sure that the music we play corresponds to the events that really deserve attention. That way our soul becomes a place of worship where the glory of Christ is always savored and its influence felt. What spiritual sounds are emanating from your heart?

Joy is a confession of faith that is not merely intellectual but tangibly emotional and experiential. A large part of the Christian life is getting to the point where our emotions reflect objective truth, and joy does this powerfully. Choosing joy is like placing a magnifying glass over beautiful things rather than ugly things and insisting not only on looking at the good but getting excited about it. Joy says God's gospel is the Big Thing and deserves our attention, and this is true even if the earth falls apart (Ps. 46:2). A person who seeks biblical joy is indignant at attempts to take the magnifying glass off of Christ and place it somewhere else.

All of our dark places are opportunities for shining the joyous truths of the gospel. Disorder in society, harsh home lives, weak and tottering churches—all are places in which to shine light. This means hardship and setbacks are actually opportunities to assert His greatness. It may be hard to orient yourself to the thought, but what better way to glorify Him than to lift up your head in the valley where shadows lurk and say, "Praise God for Jesus Christ. I am not afraid. Look what God has done for me."

You may feel the need to rejoice in the dark valley but feel intimidated about doing so. If you want to fuel biblical joy so that it shines more in the dark, remember that joy is Word-centered. Read Scripture and sound theology, looking for reasons to be and remain joyful. Make it your goal to have redemptive truth in the forefront of your heart and mind—truth you can quickly brandish like a torch in a cave, when joy must transcend a fallen world. Our Bible study and reading should be expeditions into God's sacred country that bring back dazzling fires from heaven to illumine the shadowlands.

Dark Things Even in the Word

Once we seek to kindle our joy with the Word, we encounter a difficulty that is found in Scripture itself, though the problem is not the Bible's but our own. We discover that much of the Bible hardly seems joyful at all. It is full of judgment, death, enigmas, and moral failures, and it can even seem to foster guilt and fear.

Here are just a few of the challenges: God tells Adam and Eve, "The day that you eat of it you shall surely die." The man and woman fail and transgress God's law. An angel with a flaming sword cuts off the way to eternal life. Lot chooses to live in Sodom, where his children are corrupted. Dinah is raped, and her brothers go on a revenge-spree and wipe out the Shechemites. Babies are thrown into the Nile River. God's people desert Him en masse on many occasions. The ground opens up to swallow people. God commands Israel to wipe out a whole nation for its sins. Moses is barred from the Promised Land. Saul loses the Spirit and gets an evil spirit instead. David's family is judged because he committed the terrible sins of adultery and murder. In the Prophets God writes chapter after chapter explaining all the ways He plans to destroy various nations. We're told that there is a fiery Gehenna where the worm never dies.

There are a lot of things in the Bible that many people find hard to reconcile with joy. If we don't find the good news about Christ in our Bible, it could drive us to despair. Even many Christians who read it stick to the Psalms and parts of the New Testament. But avoiding any part of Scripture is like leaving a letter from a friend unopened and unread. It won't do to turn a deaf ear to what God has said. Besides, the Bible contains sobering things because it is telling the truth about the world. Dark things appear in the Word because there are dark things in the world. But that doesn't make it any easier to rejoice when reading them.

The question before us is this: Once I finally realize that biblical joy is Word-centered, how do I find joy by reading a book that frankly seems just as dark as the world in which we live, particularly when I keep struggling against the darkness in my own soul? How can I kindle happiness in God when I read so many stories about Him being offended by evil and bringing judgment? I think more people are bothered by these questions than we, and perhaps even they, realize. We'll begin exploring the gospel answers to these questions in the following chapters.

Study Questions

1. The chapter defines biblical joy by explaining several of its qualities; list these qualities and support each with Scripture.

2. Have you resisted the idea that biblical joy is an emotion God commands us to have? Why? What are some reasons the chapter gives for why a person might resist it? Are there some Scripture passages that help us see that it is in fact an emotion?

3. How can we "rejoice in the Lord always" when there are other valid and necessary emotions?

4. How would you answer someone who says, "I rejoice in Christ when I see creation's beauty. I don't need to read about Him in the Bible"?

5. Why is Christ an adequate basis for rejoicing in a sin-cursed world?

6. List some reasons why joy is so important for Christians to experience.

7. Explain what choosing joy has to do with a magnifying glass. What sorts of things do you tend to put the magnifying glass over in your life?

8. Have you ever felt discouraged by uncomfortable things in the Bible?

9. What are some things you can do to promote biblical joy in your life?

CHAPTER 2

Joy despite God's Judgments in the Earth

We know that all things work together for good to those who love God, to those who are the called according to His purpose.
—Romans 8:28

The way to have joy in dark places is to view them, and oneself, through a gospel lens. To begin doing this we must understand two essential truths. First, the purpose for which God put the Bible in our hands—it was given to draw us into covenant with Him and lovingly tend us in that covenant. Second, what it means to be in covenant with God—He is our Father who delivers us from all evil. When we understand these things, we take a very large step closer to lasting joy. Let's consider them more in depth.

The Bible: A Covenant Document

If we want joy fueled by the Bible, we must know that it was given to bring God's people into covenant with Him and to nourish them in that covenant. God gave the Bible to inform us about His glorious attributes, Christ, salvation, the church, and many other things. But His purpose for providing this information is to evangelize and edify us. He's drawing His sheep into His fold and taking care of them once they enter it. You can sense this evangelistic purpose in texts like Isaiah 45:22, "Look to Me, and be saved, all you ends of the earth!" and Matthew 11:28–30: "Come to Me, all you who labor and are heavy laden, and I will give you rest…. Learn from Me…. My yoke is easy."

It is easy to accept this thought but not allow it to have influence in your soul. When you hold the Bible, think of God reaching out a loving hand to you personally. When thinking about the Bible, we far too often just see a book about God. There is a tremendous difference between that and a book from which God reaches out to you. When you are spiritually dry and feeling your need for refreshment, turn prayerfully to the Bible, for in it God is found as the fountain of living water, pouring out blessing in Christ.

This is true of the whole Bible, not just part of it. God gave all of it, including the Old Testament, with Christian people in mind. Peter tells New Testament believers that the Old Testament prophets were serving not themselves but you when they penned the Bible under the Spirit's inspiration (1 Peter 1:12). Paul says the same thing—all the events in the Old Testament "happened to them as examples, and they were written for our admonition, upon whom the ends of the ages have come" (1 Cor. 10:11).

We Christians are tremendously privileged to have God reach out to us like this. The magnificent creator of all things humbles Himself from first to last. The Son of God made "Himself of no reputation, taking the form of a bondservant, and coming in the likeness of men" (Phil. 2:6–7). Christ girded Himself with a towel to wash His sinful disciples' feet (John 13). He will gird Himself to serve His people in the end (Luke 12:37). All of God's dealings with man involve His stooping. He "humbles Himself to behold the things that are in the heavens and in the earth" (Ps. 113:6). The whole Bible is God humbling Himself to serve His people. When we hold the Bible in our hand, we should feel the privilege that the matchless God pursues relationship with us!

Seeing God this way ought to affect how we see dark things in the Word. This caring God cannot have included dark things in the Bible for no good reason. Judgments are a backdrop to display the advantage of the gospel. They are the opposite of God's promises to believers. Being justified by faith, believers have peace with God through Christ (Rom. 5:1). No one can ever pluck believers out of His hand (John 10:28). Such promises have a luster when you sense judgment's dark backdrop. Judgments also encourage people to be honest with God. God clearly means business, and people shouldn't presume to have joy until they confess that they deserve judgment and take refuge in the gospel. Undoubtedly many people want the comfort of the gospel but have never admitted their liability to judgment and turned away from sin to Christ.

Despite God's wisdom in including judgments in the Bible, they can still unsettle believers. But we shouldn't fear that God doesn't care about us or that we are, in the end, going to hell. Nothing kills joy more than fears like that. God wants believers to *know* that they have eternal life (1 John 5:13) and to live in the joy of that security (John 10:28–30).

When we consider the reality of God's judgments, we must remember the covenant document in our hands. God gave it to bring us into relationship with Him and to tend us like the kind shepherd that He is. The Bible's main message is the gospel, that Christ propitiated God's wrath which we deserved (Rom. 3:25). The Good Shepherd gives His life for the sheep. God's judgments are not aimed at those who repent and believe. God is your Father, and He vows to use His omnipotence to "preserve you from all evil" (Ps. 121:7).

Understanding Judgments as a Child of God

Once you're in God's fold, you must think on what it means to be there. When you come across judgments in the Bible, read them as what God will never do to His children but only to the wicked. Romans 8:28 gives you an objective basis to expect that good things are ahead: "We know that all things work together for good to those who love God, to those who are the called according to His purpose." In it, and other verses like it, God proposes a crucial thought—that you, believer, should reframe the curses and threats as positives to you. God cannot curse someone whom He has promised to bless always. When you encounter a judgment in your reading of the Word or in your experiences in the world, ask, "What is the opposite of this?" The answer is what God is giving you.

Let's say your Bible reading has brought you to the little book of Obadiah. You resist the temptation to skip it, so you begin reading and discover that the book is about God announcing terrible doom on the ancient nation of Edom because it gloated when Jerusalem was ransacked. But you are not an Edomite, so you are unconcerned and maybe a little puzzled until you reach this verse: "The day of the LORD upon all the nations is near; as you have done, it shall be done to you; your reprisal shall return upon your own head" (Obad. 1:15). You realize that He's threatening not only Edom but "all the nations." It occurs to you that God's judgment on the Edomites is a sample of what He will do to all who sin. If we've sinned, God will return it on our own heads.

Warnings like that pop up in all sorts of passages, even "safe" places like the Psalms: "You render to each one according to his work" (62:12). Believers who read and understand may get disturbed. They sense God's judgment, meted out both in time and in eternity, and know they deserve it. The emotional fallout can go in wrong directions—they may think hard thoughts about God.

But here is where the glory of the gospel comes in. Romans 8:28 tells us that nothing can ultimately harm us if we are believers in Christ. God really does vow to use His omnipotence to deliver you from all harm (Ps. 121:7). Edom is being denounced in severe terms for hating God's people; but look at your own life. Unlike hateful Edom, God has worked in you a love for His people. As a believer you are part of God's church, which He protects like the apple of His eye.

Your conscience may want to stay in the dark place: "But you've disobeyed; you deserve wrath." That's true. But Christ your head obeyed perfectly. His perfect righteousness is imputed to you (2 Cor. 5:21). Romans 8:28 therefore is true for those who find rest in Christ. When you keep the gospel in mind, reading about judgments in Obadiah causes you to sense God's wrath against sin, but then you refresh your faith in Christ, for He is the only refuge from it. If you respond this way, encountering a judgment leads you not to fear but to the reaffirmation of your basis for unconquerable joy. You can and should experience joy all over again.

The Reformer Martin Luther often struggled with fearing God's judgment. Sometimes his fears would keep him up all night long. His struggle was difficult, but he learned what it means to rely on Christ heartily. The truth influenced his soul so much that he could communicate the gospel in striking and powerful ways. Listen to him joyfully dispel darkness with a flood of gospel light, and let that light flood your own soul:

> I may boldly glory of all the victory which [Christ] obtains over the law, sin, death, the devil, and may challenge to myself all His works, even as if they were my own and I myself had done them. Therefore, when the law shall come and accuse you that you do not observe it, send it to Christ and say "There is that man who has fulfilled the law; to Him I cleave. He has fulfilled it for me and has given His fulfilling to me." When it hears these things it will be quiet. If sin comes and would have you by the throat, send it to Christ and say "As much as you may do against Him, so much right shall you have against me, for I am in Him, and He is in me." If death creeps upon you and attempts to devour you, say to it "Good mistress Death, do you know this man? Come, bite out his tooth. Have you forgotten how little your biting prevailed with Him once? Go to! If it is a pleasure to you, encounter Him again…. I pertain to this man; I am His, and He is mine, and where He abides, I will abide. You could hurt Him nothing, therefore let me alone." From this we may easily understand what kind of works they are that make us entire and righteous before God. Surely they are the works of another.[1]

I encountered that remarkable statement many years ago, and it was an important step in my comprehension of just how great Christ's salvation really is and what an excellent basis Christians have for perpetual joy. Another writer, Charles Bridges, said, "Lie not against

---

1. Martin Luther, Sermon on John 20:24–29, quoted in Horatius Bonar, *The Everlasting Righteousness* (1874; repr., Edinburgh: Banner of Truth, 1993), 76–77. This quote has been very lightly edited to remove archaic spellings and smooth out awkward punctuation.

the truth by allowing your countenance to display gloom."[2] That gets to the heart of the matter quite nicely. Joy is a matter of telling the truth about Christ to ourselves and then insisting our emotions, and even our faces, respond in agreement with that truth.

The truth is that God has gathered believers as sheep into His fold and delivered them from all disaster, including His judgments. Whether we encounter judgments in the Word or in the world, we must dispel fear with the light of God's promise, as Luther did so powerfully. God has told us to rejoice in Christ always! When we find a dark place of judgment, the gospel sheds light and ministers joy.

---

2. Adapted from Charles Bridges, *Proverbs* (1846; repr., Edinburgh: Banner of Truth, 1998), 274.

Study Questions

1. What does it mean that the Bible is a covenant document? What passages teach this idea? How should this make you feel about the Bible and the judgments in it?

2. How must God's children understand His judgments?

3. Do you believe that God will never curse someone He has promised to always bless? How should this truth affect your soul?

4. How can a person have joy if they think God might end up cursing them?

5. How can you dispel darkness and negativity better in your life?

6. How did Martin Luther respond to fears about the law, sin, death, and the devil?

7. Do you really feel like God loves you? Have your emotions learned to harmonize with the assurances of the gospel? Take a look at some of those assurances again (Rom. 5:1; 8:1, 28, 35; Ps. 23:6; Jer. 31:3). What do these assurances have to do with joy?

CHAPTER 3

Law and Conviction Necessary for Joy

The law was our tutor to bring us to Christ, that we might be justified by faith.

—Galatians 3:24

God wants believers to be convicted of sin, even after they are saved. He tells believers to "lament and mourn and weep" when they sin (James 4:9). Yet He also says to rejoice always (Phil. 4:4). Many people wonder how they can experience both joy and conviction without downplaying one or the other.

The short answer to this question is that the law's conviction is a gateway to joy. "Joy" that avoids conviction is not biblical. David prayed, "Make me hear joy…that the bones You have broken may rejoice" (Ps. 51:8). God didn't literally break David's bones; the breaking refers to the crushing conviction of sin he experienced. David wanted this conviction to lead to forgiveness and then to joy. Jesus also taught that conviction leads to joy: "Blessed are you who weep now, for you shall laugh" (Luke 6:21).

You can't ignore conviction and expect joy. Tolerating sin while "rejoicing" in the promises is the basis not for joy but only for a guilty conscience. The Bible offers no assurance or joy to unrepentant rebels. We must allow God's law, and the judgment it threatens, to bring conviction home to our conscience. We must not view law and conviction as "dark places"; instead, we should welcome them. Below are four principles that show how law and conviction lead to biblical joy and are necessary for it.

Law and Conviction Necessary for Biblical Joy

First, law and conviction lead to salvation and therefore to joy. "Godly sorrow produces repentance leading to salvation" (2 Cor. 7:10). Jesus said there is no salvation without repentance: "Unless you repent you will all likewise perish" (Luke 13:5). How important therefore to let God's law convict you! Don't smother conviction, or distract yourself from it, or medicate your guilt, or justify yourself by comparison with others. Let God's law showcase your sin. Be dismayed, not dismissive. As Thomas Watson wrote, "The oil of joy is poured chiefly into a broken heart."[1]

God's laws show us how we fall short. If you read "love is patient, love is kind" and realize that you are impatient and harsh, do not ignore these norms or presume you are "good enough." Repent before God. Doing so is honest about yourself and honoring to the law. If you read "be quick to listen, slow to speak" and realize you are actually slow to listen and quick to speak, do not rush past conviction to say, "Well, Jesus forgives me." Rushing to joy at the expense of conviction actually ruins joy because your conscience isn't easily tricked by presumption. It twists like a worm and makes you uneasy. Instead, see yourself as perpetrating evil. Accept that word *perpetrate*. Feel remorse. Confess your sin as evil, instantly humble yourself, and repent before God. I once heard a Bible teacher advise people to "let God's law land" on their consciences. Don't dodge the blow. Let it land. Your conscience will detect your honesty about sin, and your heart will be free to experience joy.

Second, law and conviction lead the sinner to Christ. Jesus said, "Come to Me, all you who labor and are heavy laden" (Matt. 11:28). Paul taught that "the law was our tutor to bring us to Christ, that we might be justified by faith" (Gal. 3:24). Once you own your sin and loath it, don't do the things so many people do: wallow in misery, "let time mend your wounds," work harder at being good, or

---

1. Thomas Watson, *The Doctrine of Repentance* (1668; repr., Edinburgh: Banner of Truth, 2016), 102.

think of repentance as all there is to conversion. Seek for the only true solution—Jesus Christ.

How is Christ the solution to being convicted by the law? He perfectly kept the law for you and paid the penalty for your sin on the cross. His righteousness is your own if you believe (1 Cor. 1:30). His death was in your stead. All your guilt was laid on Him (Isa. 53:6). He rose to confirm the power of His death to save you (Rom. 4:25), and He ever lives to intercede for you (Heb. 7:25).

When you are convicted of sin, anchor your heart to these ministries of Christ. Rejoice that Christ's work completely dismisses all your sin and the wrath of God against you. "There is therefore now no condemnation to those who are in Christ Jesus" (Rom. 8:1). The relief of this becomes palpable and life-changing if you've experienced conviction. Conviction shows us we're not the answer and points us to the One who is. This naturally leads to joy in Christ as you see how precious He is.

Third, we should still be convicted even after salvation. Justification by faith is a onetime experience and cannot be repeated or lost (John 10:28–30). But fleeing to Christ out of conviction of sin must be practiced continually, and therefore joy should be experienced continually.

The apostle John told people who were already Christians that they should confess their sins (1 John 1:9). Jesus told Peter that he still needed to have his feet washed, even though believing Christ's Word had washed his whole body (John 13:10). Therefore, flee to Christ often, whenever conviction strikes you, and rejoice anew.

Thinking that conviction pertains only to the beginning of the Christian life is a sure way to feed sin and starve joy. Repenting whenever you sin means you are aware of remaining sin and humbly sense your need of grace. You prize God's holiness and are disturbed by doing anything against His honor. You fervently pray and take continual refuge in Christ. Taking sin seriously leads to seeking Christ earnestly and rejoicing in Him greatly.

Failing to repent whenever you sin says the opposite of these things: it shows you are hard toward God, insensitive to your sin, and don't value Christ. Preachers used to speak of "keeping short accounts with God," by which they meant not allowing sin to pile up and hinder relationship with God but rather confessing and repenting whenever you are aware of sin. This attitude is not a denial that we are safely in God's kingdom by faith in Christ, as if by keeping short accounts we are keeping ourselves saved. No, keeping short accounts is necessary for maintaining a healthy relationship with God. Not keeping short accounts builds relational walls between you and God: "If I regard iniquity in my heart, the Lord will not hear" (Ps. 66:18). Joy then withers. Keep short accounts and flee to Christ whenever conviction strikes. Without this sort of lifestyle, any joy we may have is borne of a prideful heart. We must humbly repent, and then our joy will not dishonor Him.

Fourth, the law has no threat of doom left in it for repentant believers. Once you find rest in Christ, view the commands as no longer carrying the threat of death. You are free to welcome God's commands as your delight. You are free to seek to obey them by the Spirit without fear of judgment, for you cannot be condemned and are truly safe in Him (Rom. 8:1, 38–39).

Some people get hold of this gospel implication—that there is no threat left in the law—and therefore begin to dismiss the law altogether. It is important to welcome God's commands rather than dismiss them. Paul told Christians that "keeping the commandments of God is what matters" (1 Cor. 7:19). John said, "This is the love of God, that we keep His commandments" (1 John 5:3). God wants the law not only to convict us (causing us to run to Christ) but also to teach us the way of righteousness once we've run to Him. The Puritan Samuel Bolton said it quite memorably: "The law sends us to the Gospel for our justification; the Gospel sends us to the law to frame our way of life."[2]

Once people realize that the gospel doesn't erase the law but rather empowers them to obey it, they might begin to feel it is an

---

2. Samuel Bolton, *The True Bounds of Christian Freedom* (1645; repr., Edinburgh: Banner of Truth, 2010), 72.

elaborate trick to control them. The gloom of keeping rules has returned! But our relationship to the law should not be an unhappy bondage. We should love the thought of commands, not hate them: "Oh, how I love Your law!" (Ps. 119:97). Joy comes when we frame our lives by the law, realizing that we can no longer be condemned by it since we are justified by faith in Christ. There is hardly any greater news than to hear that the law, which condemned us for failing to keep it, is now an eternal friend. We will inevitably fall short of it, but Christ has made up for our lack, and we can keep striving by God's grace to improve. In Christ the law is a guide and friend and no longer condemning.

In summary, don't ignore the commands of Scripture or the conviction they bring. As you read commands and experience conviction, renounce sin once more and run to Christ, who bore your curse for you. Biblical joy results from being honest before the law, seeing oneself as hopeless, and firmly taking hold of Christ.

Warnings

It's inevitable that more warnings will be raised; there are many ways of going astray in understanding our relationship to God's law and the conviction it brings. The following caveats address some of these problems.

Beware of becoming overzealous about sorrow. When people stop avoiding conviction and begin valuing it, they can end up over-emphasizing sorrow for sin. This problem arises because people begin to wonder if their repentance is good enough. Sometimes in past ages, when societies were generally more serious about God, people even thought that they must have a certain amount of moaning on their face before they had the right to think they were saved. It is easy to laugh at such thoughts in our day, for we have nearly the opposite problem and many of us could do with a good dose of sorrow. But regardless of our culture's problem, this error thinks of repentance as savior instead of Christ. If you fear that you haven't been sorry enough for your sins, realize that the Bible does not say that your acceptance with God is based on perfect repentance.

Honestly confess your sin with genuine sorrow and then rejoice in the only perfect One, Jesus Christ. Keep your eyes on Him, and don't allow yourself to fixate obsessively on your own performance.

Beware of allowing fear of antinomianism[3] *to cause you to resist finding peace in the gospel.* Some people are suspicious of joy, fearing they might abuse God's commands. As long as you repent of your sin and flee in faith to Christ, you are not wrong to think of God's laws as holding no terror. Rather, you are doing as you must—you are insisting on relating to commands as a child of God, for your fate is not uncertain (John 10:28–30). To relate to God any other way is to disbelieve the gospel as it is revealed to us. To those of you who think in terms of imperatives, you must rest in Christ and feel loved forever, not fear damnation; in short, you must accept the graciousness of the gospel as it is revealed to us. To do anything less is suspicion of the gospel. Yes, many people are presumptuous, but don't let proponents of cheap grace keep you from resting in true grace.

Beware of presumption. What if you realize you've been presumptuous and have never truly come under conviction of sin? If you are in fact an unbeliever, the answer is the same as it is for a believer who is under conviction: repent and believe the gospel. The difference is that an unbeliever is doing it for the first time and is fleeing the very fires of hell. Read the Gospels and all the encouragements to come to Christ. I love the story of Bartimaeus, who sat by the road begging. When Jesus came by he called out repeatedly, "Jesus, Son of David, have mercy on me!" (Mark 10:47–48). That cry is tender and insightful. Bartimaeus knew his great need and set his heart on Christ to meet it. Christ's response is the best part of the story. Though others told the man to be quiet and not bother the teacher, Jesus called him to come to Him and be healed. Elsewhere Jesus said that He always responds to such people this way: "The one who comes to Me I will by no means cast out" (John 6:37). Let these assurances from the

---

3. An attitude that presumes to dismiss the law based on a misunderstanding of freedom in the gospel.

Gospels encourage you to come to Christ, whether for the first time or the millionth.

Believers have the strongest basis for joy imaginable. God has promised that goodness and mercy will follow them all of their days and they will dwell with Him forever (Ps. 23:6). Believers' attitudes to the law should not contradict the joy of such promises; they should not fear damnation because of their failures to obey it. Without the gospel, law and conviction really are dark places—pits of guilt, hopelessness, and fear. But in light of the gospel, they are gateways to everlasting joy, for they lead us to the strong tower of Christ, who will never cast us out. We must come expecting to find joy, for true joy comes through allowing the law to convict us and lead us to our Savior. And once we've come to Him, let Him lead us gently back to the law for instruction on how to live, this time without any threat or condemnation.

Study Questions

1. Why do law and conviction lead to biblical joy? What are the four answers the text gives? Support them with Scripture.

2. What are some ministries of Christ that show He is the only true solution to sin?

3. Have you ever come under conviction of sin? Can you recall times when you were convicted?

4. Is there any threat of doom left in God's law for believers? How do you know?

5. What do you think of Samuel Bolton's comment: "The law sends us to the Gospel for our justification; the Gospel sends us to the law to frame our way of life"?

6. How might an overemphasis on sorrow for sin be a problem?

7. How might fear of antinomianism be a problem? If you are afraid of abusing God's law, what might you think of the gospel?

8. How would you counsel someone who realizes he's never truly come under conviction and has been presumptuous?

9. What Scripture passages assure repentant believers that their fate is not uncertain but has been eternally decided and settled?

CHAPTER 4

Joy despite Fears
of Spiritual Deterioration

He who has begun a good work in you will complete it until the
day of Jesus Christ.

—Philippians 1:6

When you read Scripture, you are bound to encounter people's awful sins. You'll read about the horrible incident of Lot and his daughters (Gen. 19), the hair-raising account of Judah and Tamar (Gen. 38), and Israel's constant rebellion (e.g., Ex. 32). Then there is the cycle of repentance, corruption, and bondage in the book of Judges (Judg. 3:1–4). And don't forget David's sin with Bathsheba (2 Sam. 11). Bad examples abound in our own experience too. We've all been disappointed by a leader's fall into sin or demoralized by a friend's sinful choices.

Encountering these dark things may challenge your joy. It's depressing to see a person you admired fall into sin. You can become a cynic, or you might become terrified for yourself. You might fear that you'll degenerate into a downward spiral like people in Judges. You might think, "If David could fall as bad as he did, who am I to think I can stand?" Such thoughts are healthy warnings to people who rely on their own strength to serve God, like Peter did early on (Matt. 26:33). But those who have walked a bit further down the path are not confidently self-reliant as Peter was. They know the intensity of their desires and the weakness of their will. Bad examples, like David's, combined with an admittedly weak flesh might tempt them to see their whole future, and even their eternal state, as in doubt.

Though they look different, there's an ironic similarity between the boaster and the terrified. They both think that progress in sanctification depends on themselves. The one who is self-reliant thinks so and responds, "I can." The fearful thinks so and says, "I can't." But they both view themselves as alone or independent. They need to learn that God is present with believers to bless them, and the gospel provides decisive empowerment in the fight against sin. We must not think or feel as if God's help hasn't arrived yet. It has. We must rely on what He has already accomplished in Christ through the Spirit, not on our own performance.

When you encounter the dark places of others' depressing sins, view them from the gospel perspective about empowerment—Christians are people who have been equipped by the Spirit and the Word (Ps. 119:11; 2 Tim. 3:17; Gal. 5:16). Believers must not view themselves as forlorn, bereft of help, and about to fall permanently into the moral cesspool at any moment. Awful sins are what God gave the Spirit to combat and overcome. When we fear that we will deteriorate spiritually, we must seek the filling of Christ's Spirit, whom God gave to be the gracious antidote to the flesh.

For Believers, Commands Are Also Promises

God's help to believers is so powerful that His commands against sin should be understood as His promises that they will overcome it. That is quite an idea. Think of it this way—God obligates Himself to work obedience into His children. He promises to do it. This means that every time we come across a command, we are finding a goal God determines to fulfill in us, which He achieves substantially in life and completely in eternity. This truth provides help for Christians who lose their joy due to fear of spiritual degeneration. God's power guarantees we'll make progress in sanctification.

Consider the following Scripture passages which demonstrate the reality that God's commands to believers are also promises to them. Let your faith grow strong on these promises of what God says He will be and do for you. After we look at the Scripture passages, we'll address the need to reckon them as true and how we should respond if we're not living up to their promised empowerment.

First, God promises to cause us to obey. "I will put my Spirit within you and cause you to walk in My statutes, and you will keep My judgments and do them" (Ezek. 36:27). Another prophet echoes Ezekiel, where God assured Israel, "Your fruit is found in Me" (Hos. 14:8). Did you catch the marvelous thing God promises in these texts? He promises that He will generate our fruit and accomplish our obedience. That is truly remarkable.

But someone might question whether these Old Testament texts apply to New Testament believers. To answer briefly, what Ezekiel describes is also experienced by New Testament Christians (e.g., Phil. 2:13). Also, the apostle Paul lays the question to rest in 2 Corinthians 3:3 when he uses the language of Ezekiel 36:26–27 to describe the Christian experience. This means that God is active in us. It doesn't guarantee that believers will not struggle or fail. It does mean that they can expect growth, not degeneracy, and can look forward to complete victory at their glorification.

Second, God promises to put the fear of God in our hearts in such a way that precludes our falling away from Him. "I will make an everlasting covenant with them, that I will not turn away from doing them good; but I will put My fear in their hearts so that they will not depart from Me" (Jer. 32:40). What a staggering promise! John Flavel commented on this verse, saying, "That part of the promise is easily believed, that he will not turn away from us to do us good: all the doubt is of the inconstancy of our hearts with God, and against that danger, this promise makes provision."[1] God promises to use His power to transform our hearts so that they will not stop fearing God. This leaves no room for living in dread about degenerating and corrupting and falling away.

Third, God promises to make us willing and able to please Him. "It is God who works in you both to will and to do for His good pleasure" (Phil. 2:13). What a basis for confidence that we will not dry up

---

1. John Flavel, *The Method of Grace* (repr., Grand Rapids: Baker, 1977), 60.

and blow away spiritually! God has us in His hand, and we can't be plucked away; He has us there not just to protect us but to empower us. He literally provides the internal, spiritual resources that enable us to obey Him. He is "working in you what is well pleasing in His sight" (Heb. 13:21). We are not alone in our striving to make progress in the Christian life. If we were, there would be a reason to fear that we might give up, give in, and be corrupted. But God is with us, working in us, empowering us to desire to follow Him, enabling us to actually carry out that desire.

When you find sins and bad examples in the Word and in the world, remember this—these are all sins God has empowered you to overcome. When you read of David's adultery, for example, you ought to recoil and sense your own tendency to various sins, then immediately flee to Christ and rejoice that He gave His Spirit to empower you to live for Him. When you read the book of Judges and behold the habitual degeneracy of Israel, remember that God promises you will not follow that horrible pattern, for He says He will continue the good work He has begun in you until the day of Jesus Christ (Phil. 1:6). The normal Christian life is one of empowerment and growth, not degeneracy and evil.

Experiencing Empowerment

We must trust these promises without doubt or hesitation if we want to experience the power they speak of in our lives. Empowerment comes when you rely on God's promises to provide it. Paul explains this in Romans 6. Take a few seconds to follow Paul's train of thought. Believers have union with Christ; they "have been united together in the likeness of His death" (v. 5). This union empowers us, "that we should no longer be slaves of sin" (v. 6). A few verses later Paul says we must rely on that empowerment: "Reckon yourselves to be dead indeed to sin, but alive to God in Christ Jesus" (v. 11). *Reckon* means "to take something into account or consider it to be true." Paul then says, "Therefore do not let sin reign in your mortal body" (v. 12). In short, Paul is saying, "You're united to Christ; therefore, do not let sin reign." Now that we're empowered, we must use that power.

Are you distressed because you are not experiencing the empowerment that these verses tell us is the normal Christian experience? Perhaps you are not relying on God's means. If you think of obedience as just you alone with God's commands, you are over-emphasizing your personal performance and downplaying your need of His empowering promises. Look back through the teaching of this chapter and consider the biblical texts. If we neglect God's means of empowerment, it's no wonder we are like a paper tiger. We may look fierce, but the slightest breeze blows us over.

If you are disempowered, being blown about like a feather in the winds of your lusts, you may be either a non-Christian or a backslidden Christian. But whether you are a backslidden believer or an unbeliever, you need to repent of your sin and flee to Christ for forgiveness and Spirit-filling. Once you are filled with the Spirit, you can oppose the flesh and refuse to fulfill its lusts (Gal. 5:16).

Sometimes it is difficult for people to understand how to make use of God's means. It essentially comes down to believing in and seeking God's promises in your case. If you have trouble knowing what that looks like, think of all the people in the Gospels who were at the end of their rope and ran to Christ for help, believing that He could and would save them. All those stories are in the Bible to show us over and over that the same is true for us—the answer for the helpless, the demon-possessed, the blind, the deaf, the leper, and the sinful is to run to Christ. Remember the woman with the issue of blood, who crept up behind Jesus because she thought that if she could merely touch His garment she would be made well? She did touch His garment, and she was made well (Matt. 9:20–22). This story exists in the Bible not to encourage us to expect healings on demand but rather to show us that Jesus is the answer to all our needs, so we should seek Him by faith. As J. C. Ryle said so wonderfully, "If we may not touch His garment, we can touch His heart."[2] We can't locate Him on earth as the woman could, but He can still be found. He answers every repentant, believing prayer with salvation,

---

2. J. C. Ryle, *Matthew* (1856; repr., Edinburgh: Banner of Truth, 2001), 89.

and He promises significant empowerment over sin to believers who
seek Him for it. If your need is a physical ailment, He doesn't promise deliverance from illness in this life. But if you are enslaved to
sin, He does promise substantial empowerment through the Spirit,
though not total freedom from sin in this life (1 John 1:8). But as
we've seen from Romans 6, there is no reason for believers to remain
in the shackles of sin and lust.

Turning to and relying on the promises of Christ and the Spirit
is the first step to breaking the chains of sin. Once a person is firmly
trusting in God's means of empowerment, hiding Scripture in
the heart empowers a gracious soul to desire good and reject evil
(Ps. 119:11). As John Calvin wrote, "We are well fortified against the
stratagems of Satan when God's law is deeply seated in our hearts."[3]
Storing up God's Word means memorizing it, meditating on it, hearing it, praying it, and talking with others about it. Then it begins to
leap to mind, influencing our responses and shaping our emotions
and desires.

When you gain empowerment and are no longer a slave to your
sins, you'll have the joy God intends for you. People who never
gain victory are failing to live up to the promises of the Spirit and
have reason to fear. You *must* grow, but seek growth through God's
means—with Christ in your eye, His Spirit in your soul, and His
Word in your heart.

Whenever you come across depressing examples of sin, grasp
hold of the promises and once more rejoice in all that Christ has done
for you. Seeing the dark places of people's failures is an opportunity
to refresh your faith in the gospel. You should go on your way trembling at the weakness of your flesh, but you can also cling to Christ
and experience a tremendous basis for joy, for there is no lack in
Him. If you indeed were on your own, you ought to be terrified at the
certainty of your spiritual deterioration. But Christ has been exalted
as head over all things for the benefit of His church (Eph. 1:22). He

3. John Calvin, *Commentaries*, vol. 6, *Psalms 93–150* (Grand Rapids: Baker,
1999), 1:409.

ever lives for you (Heb. 7:25). He is a friend that sticks closer than a brother. He tenderly cares for each lamb in His flock. He will uphold and strengthen you till the end. If you cling to Christ, you can be assured that though you may struggle and even experience chastening, God will "keep you from stumbling" and "present you faultless before the presence of His glory with exceeding joy" (Jude 24).

Study Questions

1. Have you ever been demoralized by a friend's bad example? Describe what happened and why it demoralized you.

2. What Scriptures teach that Christians have been equipped by the Spirit and the Word? Have you tended to rely on yourself rather than on God's Holy Spirit for growth in sanctification? If so, how has that self-reliance shown itself in your life?

3. How does relying on yourself for spiritual growth affect joy? Why does it affect joy that way?

4. How does it affect you to know that God has given the Spirit to counteract the flesh and empower believers to lead a godly life?

5. List several passages which teach that every command is a goal God sets to accomplishing in the believer's life.

6. How does it make you feel to know that God Himself works in us to produce our obedience?

7. Do you believe God provides power against sin now? How might a person live who didn't believe this?

8. Does God's empowerment mean that we can expect complete victory over sin in this life?

9. How might you counsel someone who isn't experiencing the empowerment God promises in the gospel?

CHAPTER 5

Joy from Empowerment and Even Chastening

If you are without chastening, of which all have become par-takers, then you are illegitimate and not sons.

—Hebrews 12:8

As we saw in the previous chapter, it is immensely comforting to know that God is at work in our lives, keeping us from falling and continuing the good work He began in us (Phil. 1:6). If we're concerned about degenerating into evil, this promise from God's Word comes as very good news. We're not alone in our fight against sin, and we should rely on God's promises rather than depend on our own performance. But you might have another thought undermining that comfort: Isn't it true that Christians can backslide, even living in a sinful state for a long time? Such a question can diminish the comfort derived from Philippians 1:6.

Backsliding Doesn't Overcome Empowerment

We should admit at the outset that a Christian can backslide. *Backsliding* in the Bible often refers to total apostasy, which is never the fate of a true Christian (John 10:28), but sometimes it refers to a believer's slide into sin (see Jer. 14:7). We see in the New Testament that believers sometimes need to be corrected (see Galatians and 1 Corinthians). There is little doubt that a Christian can even live in sin, insensible and hardened, for a time. David did so for months (see 1 Sam. 12). In Psalm 32 he describes the experience of not confessing his sin. It drained his strength, making him weak, but then he confessed and found the relief of experiencing God's forgiveness.

We've all experienced backsliding to some degree. There have been times when our devotions grew few, our patience grew short, and our tongues grew sharp. Perhaps we hurt our family, our reputation, or even our opportunities for service.

Though Christians can backslide, it isn't wise to speculate how long they can live in such a state. The Bible does not specify how long, and it says repeatedly that the normal state of a Christian is victory over sin. "Sin shall not have dominion over you, for you are not under law but under grace" (Rom. 6:14). "Whatever is born of God overcomes the world" (1 John 5:4).

The Bible even goes so far as to deny that true Christians will persist in sin. "Whoever abides in Him does not sin [that is, "does not keep on sinning"]. Whoever sins has neither seen Him nor known Him" (1 John 3:6).

These verses may be confusing when compared with passages showing that Christians can backslide, but they make it clear that a true Christian has substantial victory over sin, though not complete victory in this life. Expecting sinless perfection now denies other important passages of Scripture (e.g., 1 John 1:8). Empowerment is what you should expect, however, and if you are not experiencing it, you must flee to Christ for His gracious filling of the Spirit (Eph. 5:18; Gal. 5:16). Empowerment over sin is the believer's birthright. Rather than make room in our lives for backsliding, we must strive to not "come short" of the promises (Heb. 4:1). Don't normalize sin; standardize victory. This glorious truth—that God's empowerment is the normal Christian experience—dramatically affects how we live.

It affects how we assess people whose lives are full of evil. If people experience no power over sin, if they have little to no inclination to do right, and if they make excuses for sin while claiming the identity of a Christian, there is little doubt about how we should view them— as very likely in need of salvation. They may conceivably be true Christians, but since we are to know them by their fruit (Matt. 7:20), believers should be deeply concerned for their soul and eternal state.

It makes us desire holiness more. When Christians truly understand what it means when Scripture says, "without [holiness] no one will see the Lord" (Heb. 12:14), they appreciate the need to take holiness seriously, especially when they realize that true Christians are empowered and have no excuse for defeat. They get serious about mortifying sin in their lives by the Spirit (Rom. 8:13). As people used to say, "The proof of the pudding is in the eating." The proof of Christians is in their fruit. If you have tolerated sin, dismissed God's commands, pointed fingers at others, and viewed obedience as optional, wake up now and see your danger. But even more, rejoice to know that God's power is available to repentant believers in Christ.

It affects how we respond to our sin. We see we have no valid reason to tolerate it. Unlike our condition before regeneration, when we were dead in sin, we are now alive and empowered against it. The moment you are aware that you have tolerated sin in your life, repent and start mortifying it by the power of the Spirit (Rom. 8:13). God gives grace to the humble, so we should admit our sin and humble ourselves before Him, praying earnestly for empowerment.

It affects our view of God, especially when we combine it with the truth that God chastens us. "For whom the LORD loves He chastens, and scourges every son whom He receives" (Heb. 12:6). Adding these two together shows that God's help is multifaceted. He empowers Christians, continues the good work in them, and chastens them when they wander. Despite appearances, God's chastening is actually encouraging. Consider two important reasons why chastisement should give us joy.

God's Chastening Is No Dark Thing

Chastening says much about God's heart for us. When you consider the way God chastens His people, it becomes clear that it could be described as doting. I don't think that word is too strong a term. Maybe *nurture* or *cherish* is better, but there is something in the word *dote* that communicates real affection and tenderness. He is engrossed in loving us. Think of it; He enables us to fight sin, diligently pouring on the help, as we've seen, but He also chastens us when we deviate. He feeds and watches but also nudges, corrects, and instructs. He is a devoted parent, providing our needs in all sorts of ways. He is not distant and aloof but instead lavishes thoughtful care on us.

When we see friends suffer chastening, or experience it ourselves, we need to see it not as God's wrath and anger, as when He judges the wicked, but as His love. Chastening should lead us to God, not drive us from Him. When reading in the Word about David's hardships after his sin of adultery, see those hardships as God's fatherly love; don't misinterpret it as God's hate. God didn't default on "goodness and mercy will follow me all the days of my life" when David fell into sin. When reading that Moses was not allowed to enter the Promised Land, remember that he was instead taken to the heavenly Canaan. Yes, chastening can be hard, but we should rejoice in it when we realize it is evidence of God's fatherly care. Every true child receives it (Heb. 12:8).

God accomplishes many important things for us through chastening. It is "for our profit" (Heb. 12:10). Chastening "yields the peaceable fruit of righteousness to those who have been trained by it" (v. 11). Many spiritual lessons cannot be inculcated by any other way than chastening; they must happen in experience, not just be communicated to us in ideas and words. This fact goes a long way in explaining why God doesn't completely empower us against sin now. We must fight the good fight of faith, wrestle and pray, mortify and deny self, fail, and learn from our failures. The experience of all this shapes our perceptions and our hearts; it teaches us to value grace and holiness in a way that nothing else can.

You may wonder, "What profitable lessons can be taught by experiencing unpleasant things?" The Puritan Thomas Watson wrote extensively on this in his book *The Lord's Prayer*, and I've summarized some of his points below.

Affliction *awakens us to the present condition of our souls.* A lazy, complacent homeowner realizes he has a hole in his roof only when he gets rained on. In the same way, affliction reveals to us the sins we have allowed to remain unopposed. Affliction *reminds us of* our past sins and *keeps us sensitive* to our weakness—we remember our forgotten evils when touched by the rod. We are reminded of our wretchedness that God has forgiven. Affliction *inspires prayer*: Watson says that "Jonah was asleep in the ship but at prayer in the whale's belly." Affliction is a *means of purging* our sins. Watson likens affliction to a medicine to cure disease and a file used to remove rust. When we're afflicted, we get busy mortifying sin. Affliction makes us *sure that we have evidences* of salvation in our lives. Without affliction we aren't as careful to produce fruit. Affliction *keeps us from pursuing earthly things* excessively. Watson says that "worldly things are great enchantments." Affliction, he says, breaks the spell that kept us enamored with earth and made us lazy in pursuing heavenly things. This is a very picturesque way of putting it. Seeing yourself surrounded by alluring siren songs that lull you to sleep, sap your will, and put you in danger should make you appreciate whatever chastening the Lord uses to raise the alarm and awaken you.[1]

A lot of wisdom is contained in Watson's writing. With such thoughts in mind, we can face the prospect of chastening with joy, assured that it is part of God's wise and loving providence. Though chastening isn't comfortable, it is but another path to joy now and forever. We must trust God and submit to His wisdom about it. He wisely sacrifices some of our comfort to develop our character, and we must be in favor of His methods. If we care most about our comfort, we'll always be bitter at chastening. But "without [holiness] no one will see the Lord" (Heb. 12:14); thank God He is determined to produce it in us! May we not kick against the goads but rather submit to His kind hand.

---

1. The points in this paragraph are drawn from Thomas Watson, *The Lord's Prayer* (1692; repr., Edinburgh: Banner of Truth, 2009), 174–75.

Study Questions

1. Though believers can backslide, the normal Christian life is one of empowerment over sin. Have you made room for, or normalized, degrees of ungodliness in your life?

2. What four effects does believing in God's empowerment have?

3. What view of God emerges when you consider that He empowers, keeps on helping, and chastens His people?

4. How does this view of God make you feel about Him, and how ought you to respond to Him?

5. Why does God not just completely empower us against sin now? Why does He allow us to persist in a partially stable condition in which we need continual help and chastening?

6. According to Thomas Watson, what does God accomplish in our lives through chastening? How do these thoughts affect your attitude about chastening?

7. Have you accepted that God is wise to use chastening and that it is not a dark thing? Can you identify reasons why you might resist the idea that God chastens those He loves? What truths from the Word might help you submit to, and find joy in, God's methods?

CHAPTER 6

Joy from the Bible's "Works-Oriented" Statements

Who may dwell in Your holy hill? He who walks uprightly.
—Psalm 15:1–2

One of the most potentially confusing and unsettling aspects of the Bible is its statements that make it sound as if people must do good works to be saved. When encountering such statements, new Christians might wonder if they believed a lie when they repented and exercised simple faith in the cross. Even seasoned believers can feel beads of sweat break out when they come across some of these statements. It is uncomfortable, no doubt about it, and it needs explaining.

Works-Oriented Statements in Scripture

Is it really true that the Bible contains works-oriented statements? Yes, it is true. Consider the small sampling below. You might be surprised that they are found in both Testaments.

> If you do well, will you not be accepted? (Gen. 4:7)

> You shall therefore keep My statutes and My judgments, which if a man does, he shall live by them. (Lev. 18:5)

> LORD, who may abide in Your tabernacle?
> Who may dwell in Your holy hill?
> He who walks uprightly,
> And works righteousness,
> And speaks the truth in his heart. (Ps. 15:1–2)

To him who orders his conduct aright
I will show the salvation of God. (Ps. 50:23)

If you want to enter into life, keep the commandments.
(Matt. 19:17)

A certain lawyer stood up and tested Him, saying, "Teacher,
what shall I do to inherit eternal life?" He said to him, "What is
written in the law? What is your reading of it?" So he answered
and said, "'You shall love the LORD your God with all your
heart, with all your soul, with all your strength, and with all
your mind,' and 'your neighbor as yourself.'" And He said to
him, "You have answered rightly; do this and you will live."
(Luke 10:25–28)

Work out your own salvation with fear and trembling.
(Phil. 2:12)

These statements obviously do not appear to harmonize well
with justification by faith alone. Some might say they contradict it.
These passages also might give the impression that salvation is by
faith and works together or that God teaches both ways of salvation
as two distinct, viable options. These are all misunderstandings.

Upon reading such verses, people have fallen into despair over
knowing the true way of salvation, over ever seeing divisions in the
church healed, over ever being able to understand the Bible. They
see only a mass of contradictions. And matters aren't helped by other
common responses: many people either ignore the problem or happily go their way with a view of the issue that they've inherited from
their faith tradition but never understood and cannot justify.

You will have difficulty rejoicing in God if you entertain even
a niggling doubt about the way of salvation. Doubts on this point
simply kill joy; they bludgeon it to death. Joy is a fragile flower that
dies when placed in the harsh environment of works-based salvation. It simply cannot sustain joy if the person believing it is honest,
for we all know we've sinned more times than we can count. If we
must appear before a holy God with our own track records, we
are doomed.

Reaffirming Grace through Faith

What are we to make of works-oriented statements in the Bible? They appear to be a dark thing in the Word that matches dark things in the world. Many religions promote works-based salvation; how can we hold on to joy if the Bible also says that salvation is by our works?

We must put all of our eggs in the one basket of justification by faith alone. The Bible repeatedly teaches that we are not saved by works but by faith alone in Christ alone. For many of us, the verses that teach this are the first ones we learned as children: "God so loved the world that He gave His only begotten Son, that whoever believes in Him should not perish but have everlasting life" (John 3:16); "For by grace you have been saved through faith, and that not of yourselves; it is the gift of God, not of works, lest anyone should boast" (Eph. 2:8–9).

If we are to believe the Bible, we must accept that we are saved "not by works of righteousness which we have done, but according to His mercy" (Titus 3:5). This is essential Christian truth. As Martin Luther said, justification by faith alone "apart from the deeds of the law" (Rom. 3:28) is the article on which the church stands or falls.

Many people accept justification by faith alone but still might feel uncomfortable, for they don't have a satisfying way to understand the "works-oriented" statements. They have a suspicion that the Bible contradicts itself and that they have just chosen the verses they personally are more comfortable with. There is nothing more destabilizing than the suggestion that one's religion is really just a self-determined concoction.

But there is a satisfying way to sort through the alleged contradiction: we must take into account that God made a covenant of works with Adam in the garden—a covenant Adam broke at the fall. This fact might be confusing at first, but it actually helps explain why works salvation isn't possible after the fall, and it also explains why works-oriented statements appear in the Bible after the fall. Let's consider these things further.

A Broken Covenant of Works in the Garden

Genesis 2 shows that God did indeed set up a works arrangement with Adam. A covenant of works is "that which teaches us justification and life by doing."[1] In the garden, "the LORD God commanded the man, saying, 'Of every tree of the garden you may freely eat; but of the tree of the knowledge of good and evil you shall not eat, for in the day that you eat of it you shall surely die'" (Gen. 2:16–17).

The arrangement is clear: If Adam disobeys, he dies; the condition is disobedience and the recompense is death. The positive recompense (a reward) is implicit—if Adam had obeyed, he would have received eternal life. This implication is borne out in Genesis 3, for after the fall, God placed an angel with a flaming sword before the Tree of Life, lest Adam "put out his hand and take also of the tree of life, and eat, and live forever" (Gen. 3:22). In other words, if Adam had obeyed God, he would have received eternal life, but he disobeyed and was cut off from life, receiving the covenant's curse, death.

A ramification of the covenant of works is found in original sin. Adam was our representative head in this covenant, so the curse of the covenant (death) also falls on us, even those of us who never broke a command, such as infants who die before they can make a rational choice (Rom. 5:12–14, 19). Adam's sin and guilt are ours, and we all are born as part of this covenant by our union with him. From Adam we receive a sinful nature and death: "in Adam all die" (1 Cor. 15:22); "We have borne the image of" Adam (1 Cor. 15:49).

Another ramification is that salvation by works is not possible now that the covenant of works is broken. Our own righteous deeds are not a viable way to eternal life—hence the angel with the flaming sword. But sinners keep hoping to be accepted into God's kingdom on the basis of their personal goodness and not the righteousness of Jesus Christ. This is to ignore the fall, our sinful natures, and our countless sins.

---

1. William Strong, *A Discourse of the Two Covenants* (1678; repr., Grand Rapids: Reformation Heritage, 2011), 90.

You may understand why works-based salvation is not possible now that the first covenant is broken, but you may wonder why God continued making works-oriented statements in the Bible after the fall.

Why "Works-Oriented" Statements after the Fall?

Asserting that God still offers salvation by works contradicts a host of Bible verses. It also contradicts the doctrine of original sin in Adam and the fact that the covenant of works is broken. That covenant is now a sure way only to eternal death (Gal. 3:10–12). Let's examine three biblical answers to the question of why God reiterates works-oriented statements throughout the Bible. These answers will show how the works-oriented statements are not a challenge to joy in Christ but rather fuel joy.

God doesn't want people to forget the covenant of works, and that is why He repeats it. Unbelievers are still under it to their doom and condemnation, so God reminds them of their own still-in-force covenant. This option fits quite well with some passages. When Jesus told the rich young ruler, "If you want to enter into life, keep the commandments" (Matt. 19:17), He wasn't offering salvation by works but simply reiterating the covenant under which the young ruler wanted to operate, for the man had asked, "What good thing shall I do that I may have eternal life?" (Matt. 19:16). Jesus was therefore answering the man according to the man's preferred system, and the system in which he was born condemned. One can see an evangelistic purpose for restating the first covenant; to be reminded of the demand for perfect obedience underscores our need of grace.

God wants people in Christ to produce good works, not to be saved but as evidence of the salvation they already have in Him. As James said, "faith without works is dead" (James 2:26). Exhorting people to prove their salvation by their works can at times sound like works salvation. For example, when Paul told the Philippians to work out their salvation with fear and trembling (Phil. 2:12), he clearly had this meaning in mind. He wasn't telling his audience to get busy and earn their way to heaven by their works. He was telling them to take fruit-bearing seriously and to get busy bearing it. So, these "works-oriented statements" aren't restatements of the covenant of works at all.

Some have said that Genesis 4:7 ("If you do well, will you not be accepted?") fits with this second option, but I cannot see it. These words were spoken to Cain, who was not a believer, so I think the first option works best in Cain's case; that is, God was reiterating the covenant of works to him as a reminder (and a warning). As you can see, sometimes it might be a bit difficult to choose between the biblical options.

Some people interpret Romans 2:6–11 with option 2:

> [God] "will render to each one according to his deeds": eternal life to those who by patient continuance in doing good seek for glory, honor, and immortality; but to those who are self-seeking and do not obey the truth, but obey unrighteousness—indignation and wrath, tribulation and anguish, on every soul of man who does evil, of the Jew first and also of the Greek; but glory, honor, and peace to everyone who works what is good, to the Jew first and also to the Greek. For there is no partiality with God.

These verses teach that people who do right receive eternal life and those who do evil receive God's wrath. On the face of it, they teach a rigid system, or covenant, of works. Perceptive readers have to reconcile the words with the rest of Scripture, and some people have used this second option to do so. Considered from the vantage of option 2, the verses refer to God rewarding fruit-bearing Christians. But the language, which speaks of God's rewarding people with eternal life for their "doing good," fits better with option 1. Paul is reminding his readers of the terms of the first covenant even as he is preparing to preach the grace of the second (in Romans 3 and beyond). One good way to encourage sinners to seek grace is to give them a good look at the original arrangement, in which all people are condemned. But it is clear that in some cases, calls to bear fruit can sometimes sound like a covenant of works. Recognizing this can help sort out confusion.

A third answer is that God repeats works-oriented statements *to point to Christ's perfect obedience.* Even in the covenant of grace God still demands perfect obedience. Christ came into the world under the law (Gal. 4:4–5), and He alone obeyed it perfectly. This leads the Bible reader to see Christ in the commandments as well as in Scripture's works-oriented statements. Where there is a command, there is Christ; He alone obeyed God's law perfectly, and He did so for believers. He is our righteousness (1 Cor. 1:30). Where there is a "works-oriented" statement, there is Christ, whose perfect works provide us with His perfect righteousness.

This turns commands into a gospel feast, and it turns obedience into a free and willing exercise of love, for we are complete in Him and need not—must not!—seek to gain God's love by our works. In Christ we already have perfect righteousness, so our obedience is to be an expression of gratitude for God's gift.

Consider how this understanding sheds light when contemplating Psalm 15, quoted above. This psalm lists all the wonderful (and for us, impossible) qualities that are necessary in order for someone to dwell with God on His holy hill. Interpreted with this third option, the psalm's demands point to the only person who ever lived up to them perfectly. Christ is our second Adam. He died in our place, but He also lived a righteous life in our place, and when we trust Him we receive a righteousness that is of God by faith (Phil. 3:9). We have Christ's righteousness imputed to our account; therefore, we can live with God on His holy hill forever, even though we deserve the opposite.

How These Answers Fuel Joy

These three options fuel biblical joy like few other truths. They help the Bible reader interpret many difficult texts and understand God's Word better. Even more, they help Christians see exactly why works-oriented statements are not dark places. There are good reasons for those legal-sounding statements in the Bible, ones that harmonize well with the gospel, and therefore Christians shouldn't be unsettled. They help believers see why they shouldn't be influenced by works-oriented statements in the world or from their own sin-influenced conscience. The world is filled with people who are trying to gain access to God by their works, and we should be fully committed to grace alone and faith in Christ alone.

Perhaps best of all, these three points, particularly the third one, help Christians see Christ in more of their Bible. When was the last time you considered a command of God and saw Christ in His moral beauty and glory? Can you behold commands such as "do not steal," or "set your mind on things above," or "don't show favoritism," or "don't engage in coarse joking," or "be slow to speak and quick to listen," and see Christ? Can you see Him in His moral perfection, as a spotless lamb? When your conscience condemns you for not keeping these commands of God, do you remember that Christ kept them perfectly and imputes His righteousness to your account? Viewed this way, every command leads you to behold Him, each command becomes provision for worshiping Him, and obedience to God not only becomes more desirable but is free from fear and coercion.

Study Questions

1. Why is a system of works-based salvation a deadly spiritual environment?

2. How do we know that God made a covenant of works with man in the garden of Eden? Give Scripture statements to support this covenant's reality.

3. What does the Scripture say about how Adam and his covenant affects us, his descendants?

4. Why is the covenant of works no longer a viable way to eternal life?

5. What are three good answers to the question, "Why does the Bible contain 'works-oriented' statements after the fall?"

6. How do these three answers help you understand the Bible better? Are there any confusing passages they cleared up for you?

7. How do these biblical answers fuel joy?

CHAPTER 7

Joy in Renouncing All Forms of Legalism

The law is good if one uses it lawfully.
—1 Timothy 1:8

At its most basic, legalism is disbelief in, even dislike toward, a gracious God. It is an exaltation of one's own goodness and a reliance on one's own performance. Legalism is a many-headed hydra; therefore, Christians must be aware of the different ways it manifests itself. It not only is complex but also can be hard to spot. As Sinclair Ferguson put it, "Legalism is a much more subtle reality than we tend to assume."[1]

Though many people misunderstand what legalism is, it is a serious danger—there is hardly anything that ruins biblical joy more. Worse, legalism is inherently anti-gospel. In its worst form it is a murderous stroke to the soul, a sort of spiritual suicide. Accepting it means putting darkness at the very center of one's life, all the while thinking very well of oneself.

Different Sorts of Legalism

A common and deadly form of legalism is *works-based salvation*, the idea that you must do good works to be declared righteous in God's sight. This is core legalism. People who suffer from it ask questions similar to the rich young ruler's: "What good thing shall I do that I may have eternal life?" (Matt. 19:16). Jesus told him to "keep the commandments" because He was answering him according to his

---

1. Sinclair Ferguson, *The Whole Christ* (Wheaton, Ill.: Crossway, 2016), 75.

own system, not because He condoned it as a viable option. God says it is a doomed way: "By the works of the law no flesh shall be justified" (Gal. 2:16).

Another form is *faith-focused legalism*, which turns faith itself into a work. This error says that faith is our goodness before God, not Christ's righteousness (Rom. 4:6; 1 Cor. 1:30). Faith-focused legalism is a "navel-gazing gospel" because it is faith looking to itself for salvation. We are indeed justified by faith alone (Rom. 3:28), but biblical faith looks away from itself to Christ. Like an anchor, faith must latch on to something (Heb. 6:19). Without a rock on which to be secured, an anchor just dangles in the water while the ship is blown out to sea.

Another form of legalism is *uncertain salvation legalism*. When people reject the doctrine of the perseverance of the saints, sometimes called eternal security (John 10:28–30), they will nevertheless still ask, "How can I have security?" Since they have accepted the idea that Christian people can throw away their salvation and potentially end up damned, their answer will naturally be focused on personal performance. They think of their obedience as necessary for retaining their salvation. The main error in this form of legalism is the same as the others—your salvation depends on your own performance.

Other forms of legalism don't impinge so much on salvation but still may be symptoms of core legalism. For example, there is *externalism*, which is an overfocus on outward standards and a de-emphasis on the state of the heart. Jesus emphasized the importance of the heart when He taught that the command against murder and adultery implied commands against anger and lust (Matt. 5:21–28). God's law rules the heart, not merely outward actions. But externalism defines sin as a matter of externals and looks away from the filth inside the cup (Matt. 23:25). Falling into this error means being an actor who makes a show of goodness while covering up inner evil.

Then there is *wrong priority legalism*: this is the tithing of mint, dill, and cumin while ignoring weightier matters (Matt. 23:23). This sort is closely related to externalism and also thinks much of its own performances, but it does so by downplaying commands that really matter for ones that are minor and easier to obey (and that don't involve repenting and mourning over sin).

Then there is *tradition-exalting legalism*. This is essentially demanding everyone conform to your particular applications to achieve "the true standard of godliness." This error is perilously close to the pride of pharisaism, canceling God's commands for one's tradition (Matt. 15:6). Once again, you can see that legalism thinks much of its own performance and also of its ability to determine the standards of performance.

There is also *self-sufficient legalism*. This views sanctification solely in terms of obedience or applying principles, without conscious dependence on the Spirit. Once again we see a preoccupation with our performance, but this time self-sufficiency is highlighted. This sort of legalist needs to come to terms with the exhortation, "Walk in the Spirit, and you shall not fulfill the lust of the flesh" (Gal. 5:16). The Word in our hand would not help us but for the Spirit in our hearts. You know you've fallen into this error if you do not feel the need for the Spirit and do not seek continual Spirit-filling (Eph. 5:18).

Let's momentarily pause our survey of the types of legalism to reflect on ourselves. If you detect in your soul even the faintest whiff of an overemphasis on your performance, then think of all you've done for God, especially the things you've done that represent you at your best, and plead with Him to accept all of it only through your mediator Jesus Christ, without whom it is refuse (see 1 Peter 2:5). Recognize that all your efforts to serve God are dung ("gilded sins" as one Puritan put it) but for Christ's sanctifying them. That is the dose of humility we all need, and it is the antidote for the poison of relying on our own performance.

At the risk of overwhelming you, let me offer three more ways legalism can reveal itself. Yes, if you can believe it, there are at least ten identifiable forms of legalism, and I'd like to encourage you to look at the Bible references mentioned so that you can see these things are indeed reflected in biblical texts.

There's *wrong-motive legalism*. Jesus said we are to deny ourselves "for My sake and the gospel's" (Mark 8:35), and this implies that people can deny themselves from some other motive. This sort of legalism doesn't have a Christocentric motive. This type of legalist obeys in order to feel good about oneself, to appear good and be accepted, to avoid fear, or merely for the sake of obedience rather than to honor and glorify God out of gratitude for His grace in Christ. Paul says to do all for God's glory, undoubtedly because it is quite easy to want glory for self (1 Cor. 10:31).

Then there is *disproportion legalism*. This error of emphasis spends more time concentrating on our works for God than on His works for us. Paul in Ephesians spends three chapters on what God has done for us in Christ and subsequently three chapters on what we should do in grateful response. Disproportion legalism rejects that balance in favor of our efforts. Not every lesson, book, sermon, or article must be perfectly balanced between faith and practice the way Ephesians is. But we must not concentrate so much on our works for God that we minimize His works for us in Christ.

Finally, there is *attitudinal legalism*. This is not forgiving others for their sins. Jesus points out that if we do not forgive, we will not be forgiven (Matt. 18:23–35). When you forgive because you have been forgiven by God, it is an evidence that you have experienced grace. Forgiveness is something that always is found, to some degree, in the heart of a Christian. People who have experienced God's grace won't deny it to others, even to those who have hurt them. To want forgiveness yet deny it to others is once again to think highly of oneself, as if it were possible to merit forgiveness while the other person doesn't merit it. Attitudinal legalism horribly poisons the life of those who suffer from it.

In short, a legalist views God as "He-whose-favor-has-to-be-earned"[2] and views himself pridefully. Legalists don't like grace; they think highly of themselves and little of others. They are very concerned to prove their worth. They tend to be unforgiving and de-emphasize the need of the Spirit. One way to know whether you have fallen into legalism is to ask some questions of yourself. Here

---

2. Ferguson, *Whole Christ*, 82.

are just a few: "Do I have difficulty forgiving others?" "Do I find it hard to rejoice when someone else is praised?" "Do I feel like God loves me more when I perform well?" "Am I far more comfortable thinking about what I am supposed to do as a Christian than what God does for me in Christ?" "Do I compare myself favorably with others and despise them?" "Do I think of Christian growth primarily in terms of exerting willpower?"

You may feel overwhelmed at all the ways legalism can crop up, but it is helpful to note its common denominator, unbelief and pride. The basic answer to the problem becomes clear: "Humble yourselves in the sight of the Lord, and He will lift you up" (James 4:10). Falling down before your gracious Lord in repentance and faith allows you to pick yourself back up rejoicing in all that Christ is for your soul. Abandoning pride frees you from the spiritual rat race of over-emphasizing your performance.

What Legalism Is Not

A common error is wanting to be known as a Christian yet maintaining a loose lifestyle; those who fall into this can respond negatively to others who want to be holy, lobbing the epithet "legalist" at those who disturb their conscience. This sad reality can popularize wrong ideas about legalism.

Here are some things that are often misidentified as legalism. Love for God's commands, highly esteeming them, is not legalism: "Oh, how I love Your law! It is my meditation all the day" (Ps. 119:97). Wanting to obey God's commands is not legalism: "Keeping the commandments of God is what matters" (1 Cor. 7:19). Expecting true faith to produce obedience is not legalism: "Faith without works is dead" (James 2:20). Knowing people by their fruits is not legalism (Matt. 7:16). Respecting all God's commandments, not just some of them, is not legalism (Ps. 119:5–6). Insisting that the Bible is the true measure of right and wrong is not legalism (2 Tim. 3:16–17).

Feeling duty bound to obey is not (necessarily) legalism. Let's expand on this one, because it is a common error to reject any sense of duty in relating with God. Christians must not be duty bound in the sense of feeling they must obey in order to be saved, as if in a covenant of works.[3] Indeed not! But Christians are duty bound, or morally obligated, to keep God's commands, because God is their Lord and master. Jesus said, "Why do you call Me 'Lord, Lord,' and not do the things which I say?" (Luke 6:46). Those who dislike duty often speak of how love ought to motivate all our actions; this is true, but love is not exclusive of duty. In fact, love strengthens it. When I loved my wife enough, I married her and made a vow to forsake all others. I put myself willingly in an arrangement of duty. If you love someone, you make yourself duty bound to them. You don't do so grudgingly but rather glory in it.

Legalism and Preaching

Preaching the law in order to convict sinners, saved or unsaved, and lead them to Christ is not legalism. Neither is preaching the law as guidance for Christian living. If a preacher says, "You must obey," he is not necessarily being a legalist. Preachers have been given a solemn task: "Convince, rebuke, exhort, with all longsuffering and teaching" (2 Tim. 4:2).

People are led to Christ when their consciences are stirred, and therefore law must be preached to lead sinners to Christ. The law shows us our disease, and the gospel brings the cure. Yet, sadly, preachers can and do fall into legalistic preaching. They can over-emphasize the law and the keeping of standards as the primary means of assurance. If a preacher concentrates on commands too much, a harsh and unlovely spirit will creep over his ministry. But preachers must remember that they are *gospel* preachers, not critics, moralizers, coaches, or pundits. They minister the new covenant and the crucified Christ while the free offer of the gospel still stands. Our ministries must be veritably drenched in good news.

Preachers must also present the law in a gospel way. Their preaching must be carried out with *gospel manners*—they should

---

3. See Samuel Bolton, *The True Bounds of Christian Freedom* (1645; repr., Edinburgh: Banner of Truth, 2010), 138–40.

not stoop to harsh speech, which contradicts the Spirit's fruit and the tenderness of the Father to His children. Their preaching must promote *gospel motives*—preachers must preach the law-keeping of believers as the way for them to glorify God and to show gratitude for Christ's salvation. It must foster *gospel assurance*—law must not be preached so as to inculcate fear and doubt in Christians. People fall into the belief that they must obey in order to assure their doubting hearts of God's love. Believers already have God's love in Christ, and obedience must flow from confidence in that. Their preaching must also include *gospel means*—law must be preached with one's eye firmly fixed on union with Christ and the indwelling Spirit for empowerment. Otherwise, people will be subtly taught that they are able to serve God on their own when God actually says, "Without Me you can do nothing" (John 15:5). How joyful preaching becomes when these things are treasured and practiced! When it is free of legalism, preaching becomes winsome, hopeful, and joyful.

How Legalism Destroys Joy

Consider just a few effects legalism has on the soul.

If you think your salvation depends on what you do or decide, then God loves you only if you perform up to a certain undefinable standard. You would naturally fear that you didn't do something well enough or didn't balance out your sins enough. Therefore, you would be uncertain of the outcome of all your efforts; you would also be tempted to be dishonest when evaluating your performance in order to calm your fears. Ultimately you will have no assurance that God loves you, because your conscience detects your dishonesty.

If you feel that your assurance depends primarily or solely on your fruit, your attention will be directed to that fruit, your works. Your attention will be on yourself, not fixed on Christ's obedient life and the imputation of His righteousness. You wouldn't rejoice at His bitter death to pay the penalty for all your sin. His intercession for you at the Father's right hand would mean little to you. Focusing on your own fruit without a clear view of Christ leaves you little better off than if you believed in works-based salvation.

If you unduly emphasize your performance, and someone sins against you, it has dramatic poisoning effects in your soul. If you don't feel loved by God and are hoping your works will be sufficient, you are constantly comparing yourself with others and promoting yourself. Now add others' sins to that. When you are graceless and others pour the poison of hate into your heart, it is impossible not to be infected and hate them in return, because you think you should be affirmed and appreciated for your good qualities, and they had the audacity to reject you. But in Christ you know that you are a miscreant God has forgiven, and your sin against Him is far greater than anyone's sin against you. You are a wretch whom God has marvelously shown grace. How can you hold grudges against other wretches, even those who mistreat you?

If you do not constantly feel the need of the Holy Spirit's empowerment, obedience then becomes all about you exerting your willpower, creating goals, making action points, and berating yourself when you fail. You'll always be trying to pump yourself up but ultimately be disappointed at your inevitable failures. How joyless! But oh, the relief of believing you can do nothing without Christ and gratefully receiving the message that God has already provided all the help that is necessary through the indwelling Spirit. You'll constantly be grateful and seeking help from His power supply.

Removing Vestiges of Legalism

There are times in life when the danger of over-relying on your performance becomes very apparent. It is easier to impress on younger people the fact that a person with true saving faith must and will produce good works. It is when you're more mature—when you've examined your fruits, even your best works—that you begin to realize that fruit should not be the primary means of assurance. Shreds of any remaining legalism fall away as your eye of faith gladly shifts to a far better person than yourself.

My wife nearly died several times in 2010. After many months of her walking on the edge of eternity, we discovered she had a very rare condition that can be fully remediated by medication that provides what normal bodies produce on their own but which her body, for some reason, had stopped producing. I'll never forget standing at the pharmacy, trembling as I held that medication for the first time, realizing I had her life in my hands. I took it home, gave it to her, and in a few hours she began to improve noticeably. It took many months, but she healed and has lived a normal life thanks to God's directing us to that medication which she must take regularly. We call it the manna in the bottle.

When my wife was at her worst, when she was confined to bed suffering after many weeks of doubt about her true condition, I realized that she really could die. I began to imagine raising my small children myself, and I thought of life without her. I watched her misery with dismay, but I wanted to minister to her and encourage her somehow in her dark place. My mind went to God's promises about fruit. At one point I told her that she was the best, most noble mere human I'd ever known—totally true; my opinion is unchanged. I told her that God had produced great fruit in her, that she ought to be assured that she was going to awaken in glory. I'll never forget what she said next from her sickbed: "No. All my works are foul. I need Jesus." Her powers of self-reflection were heightened due to her being on the brink of eternity. She saw failure and weakness in her best deeds. More than ever she realized that if she were to stand before God, she had to put all her faith in the perfect one, Jesus Christ. I was stunned by her words and never forgot them.

Recently I read of Scottish Puritan David Dickson's words on his deathbed, when his friend asked him how he was. His words remind me of my wife's experience. Dickson answered his friend, "I have taken all my good deeds, and all my bad deeds, and cast them together in a heap before the Lord, and I have betaken me to Christ, and in him I have found full and sweet peace."[4]

I'm not saying my wife was a legalist before this experience, nor was I. It is true that genuine faith produces good works (James 2),

---

4. Lightly edited quotation of David Dickson, as found in Donald Macleod, *Therefore the Truth I Speak* (Geanies House, Fearn, Ross-shire: Mentor, 2020), 392.

and it is also true that Christians must make their calling and election sure by adding virtue to their profession of faith (2 Peter 1). And we both fully understood that we are saved by faith, not works. But through this experience we learned to put fruit firmly in its secondary place as a means of assurance. I suspect many Christians need to learn this. It hit home to us that even our best works are faulty and that the primary way to assure one's heart is to look to Jesus, who is the true Light in all dark places. As the popular hymn says it so simply, "My hope is built on nothing less than Jesus' blood and righteousness."

This chapter is by no means the last word on the subject of legalism. It is an attempt to provide a lot of help in a short space. Much more could be said and has been said by others. I pray, however, that you have read enough to encourage you to ground your soul in grace and in the joy and peace that comes from believing in a loving, forgiving God. May your life be full of joy in the gospel of Jesus Christ, and may that joy lead you to greater efforts at pleasing and obeying Him.

Study Questions

1. In your own words, provide a basic definition of legalism.

2. List several sorts of legalism and the Scriptures that mention them.

3. What are the common denominators among all the sorts of legalism?

4. Have you fallen into any kind of legalism? Do you have a tendency, or bent, toward any particular type?

5. List some things that are commonly called legalism but are actually not. Which Scriptures show that they are virtues not vices?

6. How can preachers preach law without falling into legalistic preaching?

7. How does legalism destroy joy? Has legalism hindered your own Christian joy?

8. Have you learned to put fruit in its secondary place as a means of assurance? What is the primary means of assurance?

CHAPTER 8

Joy by Quieting Your Conscience in the Cross

Let us draw near with a true heart in full assurance of faith, having our hearts sprinkled from an evil conscience and our bodies washed with pure water.
—Hebrews 10:22

It is often a troubled conscience that steals our joy. Your conscience can trouble you about all sorts of things—a person who irritates you leaves the room, and you speak unkind words about him that are overheard; your eyes linger a bit too long where they shouldn't; you download content from the Internet for free even though you know it violates intellectual property rights.

Things you read in the Bible might also alarm your conscience. God seems to imply that after death there will be no blessing for rich people: "Woe to you who are rich, for you have received your consolation" (Luke 6:24). Paul says that people are cursed if they don't love Christ (1 Cor. 16:22), and you know you don't love Him enough, so you begin to fear you don't love Him at all. Proverbs explains that if you won't listen to the cry of the poor, no one, including God, will listen to your cries (Prov. 21:13). All these things, and many more, can create a lot of anxiety.

Responses to a troubled conscience can make things worse. You might wallow in fear or frantically examine fruit in your life to salve your conscience. You might run from things that provoke conscience, such as church or Christian friends. You might stifle conscience with other thoughts and activities or confidently plan to be a better person. All the while conscience still pierces like a thorn.

Even those who want to respond rightly to guilt are still profoundly affected by even a shred of it. As Thomas Watson wrote, "Guilt clips the wings of prayer so that it cannot fly to the throne of grace."[1]

Whether your conscience is troubled by a standard in the Word or by something you thought or did, your answer is to look with repentant faith to the cross of Christ. God wants our consciences to register peace, not by looking at our fruits but by looking at and relying on Christ's perfect work on the cross. God wants you to believe in the effectiveness of Christ's atonement so much that, on the basis of it, your conscience no longer feels alienated from God.

If this seems too good to be true, you need to be refreshed by the gospel. It is easy to be influenced by a subtly changed version of it that attempts to shift faith's gaze to a wrong object, such as our faith, choice, or our track record. We must constantly refresh our faith in the cross.

Christ's One Offering Perfects Believers Forever

Christ's effective atonement is the right object of your faith, and relying on His accomplished work should calm your conscience. Do you believe that a person's conscience should be perfectly at peace by faith in Christ? Or do you think you must achieve a certain level of personal holiness before peace of conscience should be allowed? These are important questions, for how you answer them says what you think of Christ's atonement. Let's take a look at the teaching of Hebrews 10 as we sort through this.

First, consider how Old Testament sacrifices were limited. They pointed forward to Christ because they could never take away sin and bring peace of conscience (Heb. 10:1–4). If animal sacrifices could have taken away sin, then worshipers "would have had no more consciousness of sins" (v. 2). "No more consciousness of sins" doesn't mean unawareness of having committed further sin, as if being numb to sin is a good thing. Indeed not. Rather, it means

---

1. Thomas Watson, *The Godly Man's Picture* (1666; repr., Edinburgh: Banner of Truth, 1992), 11.

unawareness of any sin that can be held against you and exclude you from God's family. "No more consciousness of sins" means recognizing that God has legitimately ushered in a state of complete pardon; it means really feeling that there is "now no condemnation" (Rom. 8:1).

Animal sacrifices could not provide peace of conscience because their perpetual repetition constantly reminded worshipers of their sin (Heb. 10:3). They "rubbed their noses in it" you might say. It's not that there was no salvation in Old Testament times; rather, salvation came by seeing the weakness of sacrifices and thus relying on their fulfillment—Christ, the "good things to come" (v. 1). But if animal sacrifices couldn't provide a basis for peace of conscience, what is Christ's sacrifice able to do? Though Hebrews 10 hasn't stated it outright (yet), it clearly implies that Christ's sacrifice provides a basis for peace of conscience. Before going any further, ask yourself, "Do I have peace of conscience? Is it based on Christ's sacrifice? Have I accepted Christ's perfect work as a full reconciliation?"

Second, animal sacrifices were originally intended to make way for Christ (Heb. 10:5–10). The Old Testament predicted this: "Sacrifice and offering You did not desire" (v. 5, quoting Ps. 40:6). God took away those sacrifices, which He did not desire, so He could establish Christ's perfect sacrifice (Heb. 10:9). The main point here is that the Old Testament says that God had planned on sending Christ all along. This means that God never meant for animal sacrifices to last forever. The animal sacrifices were always intended to point forward to Christ's coming perfect sacrifice.

Third, animal sacrifices can't compare with Christ's effective sacrifice (Heb. 10:11–14). Animal sacrifices were continual but perpetually ineffective; Christ's was once-for-all and perpetually effective. See how verse 14 describes the efficacy of Christ's sacrifice: "by one offering He has perfected forever those who are being sanctified." Take that in. You may wonder, in this context, what "perfected forever" means. It means that Christ's death does the opposite of the ineffective animal sacrifices. Animal sacrifices could not give a basis for peace of conscience before God (v. 2), but Christ's does. Christ's atonement is supremely effective to cleanse all sin and provide forgiveness forever.

You may never have anchored your faith on Christ's supremely effective atonement. Many Christians are used to thinking of their accepting the gospel as that which brings forgiveness. If you listen to many people give their testimony of salvation, you will hear much about the events surrounding their choice to believe and next to nothing about the meaning of Christ's death. That may tell you where their focus is. Other Christians claim that Christ's atonement doesn't save per se but renders people *savable*—if personal faith is added to the mix, then salvation occurs. But the Bible doesn't speak of Christ's sacrifice as making salvation merely possible. Hebrews 10:14 is one verse among many that provides a correction to such ideas (see also Heb. 1:3; Eph. 1:7). The cross *perfects forever.* It totally and completely saves as complete payment for *all* a believer's sin (Col. 2:14). When people begin to feel saved because of a choice they made to believe, they've begun to trust in themselves. Biblical faith puts no stock in itself but looks to Christ's cross.

I once preached through Hebrews 10, and a visitor came up to me afterward and objected to the idea that people's consciences should be at peace on the basis of Christ's cross. Such an idea would create apathy, he said. People wouldn't want to produce good works, he thought, because they would feel so saved that they wouldn't feel any pressing need to obey. He had correctly identified a genuine problem—widespread apathy and lawlessness—but he implied that the gospel was to blame. And he implied that works were best motivated by doubt, not assurance of God's love. Should uncertainty about God's love motivate our living righteously? Paul says the opposite: "The love of Christ compels us" (2 Cor. 5:14).

Are you leery of embracing Christ's effective atonement because you fear losing motivation to live righteously? If so, what should bring peace of conscience? If a person should feel peace of conscience only if they produce fruit, why does the Bible say that it is the cross of Christ alone that can provide a basis for peace of conscience before God? Are we going to encourage people to feel saved or not based on their performance? Listen to the wording again: "By one offering He has perfected forever those who are being sanctified"

(Heb. 10:14). What perfects forever? Christ's one offering. The Puritan John Owen explained how crucial it is to accept this and allow your conscience to rest in it: "The discharge of conscience from its condemning…power, by virtue of the sacrifice of Christ, is the foundation of all other privileges we receive by the gospel. Where this is not, there is no real participation in any other of them."[2]

The proper starting place in Christianity is to believe that Christ took care of all your sin, past, present, and future, at the cross. Your choice to believe, even if you understand your faith as God-given faith (as you should), does not scrub away one sin or make amends for your previous unbelief. Neither do your works, or "fruits." Only Christ does that, and He did it perfectly on the cross for all His chosen. Once you gain that clarity and accept the effectiveness of His cross, you can be free to bear fruit without doubt, in perpetual gratitude for God's great salvation. To you Christ is a full savior, and your life becomes a continual proclamation of that rather than an attempt to show yourself to be "good enough," better than others, or of sufficient godliness to feel assured about your spiritual condition. The best fruit is that which is borne of a life of joyful faith in Christ. The best obedience comes from hearts that have melted at His mercy.

To put all this in a simple nutshell, God wants your conscience to be perfectly at peace based on Christ's sacrifice alone. Look to Christ and keep looking. "Look to Me, and be saved, all you ends of the earth!" (Isa. 45:22). Faith is healthy only when it looks to God in Christ consistently. Faith in the cross "plucks the thorn out of the conscience," as John Flavel put it.[3] Where is your gaze resting?

Finally, Hebrews 10 states that we should have "our hearts sprinkled from an evil conscience" (v. 22). Clearly, it is not speaking of literal, physical sprinkling of a liquid. It is saying that Christ's blood should do to the conscience exactly what animal sacrifices couldn't do: cause worshipers to have "no more consciousness of sins" (v. 2). John Flavel interpreted "sprinkled from an evil conscience" this way:

---

2. John Owen, *Hebrews* (repr., Evansville, IN: Sovereign Grace, 1960), 6:436.
3. Flavel, *Method of Grace*, 214.

"The blood of Christ sprinkles us from an evil, that is, an accusing, condemning conscience."[4] In context that is exactly what it means. Believing in Christ's blood, apprehending it as it actually is, should free the conscience from feeling condemned before God.

How to Respond to a Troubled Conscience

How, then, do you respond when your conscience is troubling you? The truth we saw from Hebrews 10 about Christ's effective atonement points to a Christ-focused process. When you feel guilty, reject unbiblical ways of solving the problem. Do not just try harder. Don't "flagellate" yourself or think you must clean yourself up before coming to Christ. Don't just survey all the "good fruit" you've produced. And don't ignore guilt, suppress it, "brush it under the carpet," or banish it on the basis of "I accepted Jesus when I was six."

Instead, when conscience strikes, refresh your faith in Christ as your effective savior. Flee once more in repentance to your only hope, the cross of Christ. Take refuge in Him like a sheep fleeing to the shepherd when menaced by a wolf. As often as guilt menaces you, rely on His effective atonement. Insist that your conscience registers peace with God based on it and that you have a full sense of pardon. If the cross has "enough in it to satisfy God, it must have enough in it to satisfy conscience."[5]

When you realize once more that your true safety, even from that danger which is yourself, is Christ, then rejoice, for to do otherwise is to say the Shepherd cannot or will not defend you from the wolf. A frigid sense of alienation can easily creep over our souls, but when we feel safe in His arms, rejoicing in Christ warms us up toward God.

Once you are rejoicing, address whatever sin your conscience condemns you for—but without doubt in the efficacy of Christ's cross and the forgiveness it provides. Honestly admit your need to improve your Christian walk, and don't ignore sin! But now that you

---

4. Flavel, *Method of Grace*, 304.
5. John Flavel, *The Fountain of Life* (1671; repr., Grand Rapids: Baker, 1976), 319.

are rejoicing in the cross, you will be able to tackle the issue of your sin without slighting Christ's work or relying on self. Fight sin by relying on the Spirit and with buoyant faith in the Savior and His perfect work. Even if your struggle against sin goes on for a long time, keep believing that God allows your continued struggle for a good purpose—to teach you to cling even harder to the cross, to repent, to see the evil of sin, and to seek Spirit-filling for empowerment.

This is how to have joy when conscience troubles you. It points out an important logical and spiritual flow to dealing with guilt, one that keeps Christ and His cross first and central in your continued Christian experience. In short, biblical joy starts with and can thrive only on decisive and continual faith in the cross.

Study Questions

1. What are some ways people respond wrongly to a troubled conscience?

2. What are the four points drawn from Hebrews 10?

3. What does "no more consciousness of sins" mean? What doesn't it mean?

4. What does "by one offering He has perfected forever" mean? What does "effective atonement" mean?

5. Have you fallen into feeling saved based on a choice you made?

6. Do you serve God because you feel you must get God's love, or do you serve Him because you are assured you have His love based on Christ?

7. What is the right process in dealing with guilt? How does faith in Christ's effective atonement make even our continued struggle against our sin a joyful affair?

CHAPTER 9

To Have Joy
You Must Have Faith

Faith is the substance of things hoped for, the evidence of things not seen.
—Hebrews 11:1

As we live in the world, our eye of faith can become so blurry that we no longer spiritually "see" and no longer are moved by what we read in the Word. You have experienced it—the thoughts on the page seem unlovely. Nothing jumps off the page to penetrate your heart. Your heart and mind, which were once full of delight, seem dead, like a cold, sooty hearth where once blazed a cheerful fire.

We instinctively know such a state is tragic. A dead heart slights the glorious God who deserves heartfelt worship. But to maintain joy in God, one must have a keen eye of faith. Your faith must be able to "see" the truth of God and delight in it. Your faith must come out of its burrow, blink in the light of the sun, and take in God's wonders.

The Nature of Faith and Hebrews 11:1

Hebrews 11:1 has a lot to say about the nature of faith. It isn't all the Bible has to say about faith—far from it—but it is unique. It is the only place where the Lord says to us, "Let Me tell you what faith is." You can know a lot about faith even if you don't fully understand Hebrews 11:1, but this verse explains something vital about faith being a capacity of spiritual perception. But before we get to that, we need to deal with some confusion people have with the verse.

There is a centuries-old debate over Hebrews 11:1. Is faith the substance of things hoped for (KJV, HCSB), or is faith confidence in what you hope for (ESV, NIV)? Is faith substance or is it confidence? That appears to be the debate in a nutshell, and if you glance through various translations of Hebrews 11:1, you'll quickly become aware of the issue.

The difficulty is that both *substance* and *confidence* have weighty arguments against them as legitimate translations in Hebrews 11:1.

The problem with saying that "faith is the *substance* of things hoped for" is that it seems to downplay the objectivity of salvation and heaven. It seems to say that your faith is the reality of what you hope for. You might chuckle when that sinks in. If someone said that your hopes for an upcoming vacation were the substance of your vacation, you'd begin wondering if you were ever going to go on vacation at all. This translation implies that there is nothing more to spiritual realities than the faith you have in them. It's like saying, "Faith is all there is to what you hope for." Surely that is not what the writer of Hebrews meant to say.

But there is a problem with the translation *assurance* or *confidence* too. For one thing, this option is the minority report in the history of translation. The learned Puritan John Owen said that the best translators and expositors throughout church history rejected *assurance* or *confidence*.[1] A careful analysis also reveals a tautology, or a nonsense statement. Biblically, hope is confident expectation. "The things hoped for" therefore means "the things we confidently expect." To translate as *confidence* makes the statement mean "faith is confidently expecting the things we confidently expect." It is viciously redundant. This casts serious doubt on this translation, and it doesn't help to use dubious synonyms to try to make the redundancy less obvious, such as "faith is confidence in what you hope for."

Neither of the two translations stand up to scrutiny. What, then, does Hebrews 11:1 mean? We cannot make the mistake of simply passing over the difficult first part of the verse and interpret it in the light of the latter half of the verse, which appears to be less problematic. We must strive to understand the first part too.

---

1. Owen, *Hebrews*, 7:8.

Here is a third option. The human mind has the capacity to see, to give weight to. One recommended word is *realization*.[2] Another term is *substantiate*, in the sense of inwardly, or subjectively, giving things weight. This is exactly how John Owen interpreted Hebrews 11:1: "Faith gives those things hoped for a real subsistence in the minds and souls of them that believe."[3] Charles Hodge spoke similarly: faith gives to unseen things "a consistence, a visibility as it were."[4] Geerhardus Vos did so as well. "In Hebrews...faith is...the organ for apprehension of unseen and future realities, giving access to and contact with another world."[5] These three men are well known for having been very careful exegetes, and they appear to have it quite right.

Therefore, the translation would be "faith is the realization of what we hope for," or "faith is substantiating what we hope for." This is different from saying, "faith is confidence in what we hope for," because substantiating is a different (though of course related) idea than having confidence, so there is no vicious redundancy. I'm convinced that the writer to the Hebrews is saying that faith is, by nature, an inward substantiation in which spiritual things are perceived in the soul and take on reality there. It is an eye that sizes up and takes into account things that the physical eye cannot see.

Contextual Support

Before we accept this meaning, let's note that the context supports it. Noah gave weight to God's warning of the flood though he had never beheld one: "Noah, being divinely warned of things not yet seen" (Heb. 11:7). Abraham did something similar; he "went out,

---

2. Frederick William Danker and Walter Bauer, eds., *A Greek-English Lexicon of the New Testament and Other Early Christian Literature* (Chicago: University of Chicago Press, 2000), 1040, says that a good case can be made for this meaning in this context.

3. Owen, *Hebrews*, 7:8.

4. Charles Hodge, *Exegetical Lectures on Hebrews* (Edinburgh: Banner of Truth, 2019), 113.

5. Geerhardus Vos, *Grace and Glory* (1922; repr., Edinburgh: Banner of Truth, 1992), 104.

not knowing where he was going" and lived in tents (vv. 8–9). Why? Because he "waited for the city which has foundations, whose builder and maker is God" (v. 10). Sarah also did this. She inwardly substantiated God as faithful: "Sarah herself also received strength to conceive seed, and she bore a child when she was past the age, because she judged Him faithful who had promised" (v. 11). This spiritual sight is said to characterize all these people. "These all died in faith, not having received the promises, but having seen them afar off" (v. 13).

The discussion of Moses especially underscores faith as spiritual perception. Moses considered the reproach of Christ, looked toward the reward (Heb. 11:26), and saw "Him who is invisible" (v. 27). The great application of Hebrews 12:1–2 universalizes this spiritual sight as a norm for us all: "Looking unto Jesus, the author and finisher of our faith." We too must look and perceive unseen things just as our forefathers did.

This inner realization or substantiation is not merely perception. When you realize something, you do more than perceive it and become cognizant of it. You are struck by and strengthened by what is seen. Geerhardus Vos said, "Faith is not purely prospective: it enables to anticipate; it draws down the imperishable substance of eternity into its vessel of time and feeds on it."[6] Realizing and substantiating what we hope for leads to gaining inner sustenance from it, and this leads to encouragement, contentment, longsuffering, and joy.

Does Your Eye of Faith See Clearly?
And this brings us to the matter at hand. You can't have biblical joy without this perceptive, realizing faith. You have to have a bottom to your confidence, something solid on which to stand. This is especially true if the trials you face are persecutions for Jesus's sake. No one will lay down his life for a Jesus who has no more solidity in the soul than a fancy or a phantom.

Are spiritual realities real to you? Have you given them weight in your soul? Are you struck by them, "bowled over" by them, if you

---

6. Vos, *Grace and Glory*, 118.

will? Do you see them every bit as much as you see your armchair, your front door, or the face of your friend? Is your eye of faith sharp and perceptive? Do God, salvation, and heaven hold more weight in your soul than savings, investments, and retirement?

As you've read the Word's precious promises mentioned in this book, did your soul give them weight? Is it precious to you that the Bible is a covenant document and that your Father delivers you from all evil? Have you substantiated the truth that the law carries no curse for you as a believer? That God promises to continue His sanctifying work in you? That He lovingly chastens you when you wander? That the law reveals Christ's moral perfection? That Christ's atonement is so effective that your conscience ought to be completely at peace on the basis of it? It would be easy, due to our fallen natures, to simply read over these things and not "realize" them in the soul.

It is not only Hebrews that speaks of realizing heavenly things. Colossians 3:1–2 tells us to seek the things above, where Christ sits at God's right hand. Paul speaks of a spiritual activity of the soul, much as Hebrews 11 does. To seek things above, you must substantiate them, for then your soul will go out to them, dwell on them, pray about them. Paul puts it this way: "set your mind on things above" (v. 2).

Perhaps you are distressed that your "eye of faith" does not see things well enough; do you need to exercise it more? I've noticed that when I exercise physically, I enjoy beautiful things more. After a brisk walk, I look on the blue sky, a forest landscape, or sunshine on a splash of yellow leaves, and I can see them better and more clearly. The sun seems brighter, the yellow seems more yellow, and I am aware that I notice each leaf on the trees. When I see things precisely, my enjoyment of them increases. Just so, when our eye of faith is exercised, spiritual realities become clearer, and we enjoy them more. Our hearts are then drawn to God and Christ and heaven with real longing and passion. Biblical joy comes from a clear view of the Christian faith, from a good grasp of doctrine. I've often felt that a key to life is simply taking the time to enjoy biblical truth the way we enjoy a beautiful landscape. Just as we feast our physical eye on beauty, we must feast our spiritual eye on biblical doctrine, which has its own beauty.

People are often backward regarding biblical doctrine in our times. This backwardness is one of the chief challenges to my joy because I really want people to love and delight in God. To think of them being disinterested or apathetic is a thought full of grief to me. I once heard a mother lament over her wayward daughter, saying, "I wish she could be happy with Jesus." I feel this way about God's people all the time. Think of the implication of "seeing" Christ by considering doctrine—to neglect doctrine is to resist seeing Christ and rejoicing in Him.

But our eye of faith must be so acute that spiritual realities are more vivid to us than physical ones. Paul says in another place, "We do not look at the things which are seen, but at the things which are not seen…the things which are not seen are eternal" (2 Cor. 4:18).

If God, heaven, salvation, and the coming judgment were more real to us, think of the results. Temptations would lose their power to lure us. Discouragements and persecutions would lose their power to depress us. We would say with Paul, "our light affliction, which is but for a moment, is working for us a far more exceeding and eternal weight of glory" (2 Cor. 4:17). We would also rejoice. Jesus said that spiritual sight gave Abraham joy: "Abraham rejoiced to see My day, and he saw it and was glad" (John 8:56). In that statement Jesus explicitly connects perceptive faith with joy. To have joy, you must have faith.

Something about living in the world seems opposed to having an acute eye of faith. Society offers an endless supply of distractions we can absorb ourselves with that will keep us from cultivating appreciation for doctrine. This is simply a matter of our attention being elsewhere.

Modern society does more (and worse) than provide a crop of distractions. Wallowing in it kills our eye of faith or makes it so weak that it no longer can conceptualize without visual stimuli. In other words, people today have far less ability to interact with the written word and are less capable of being influenced and affected by it. If you've ever read something, then read it again and again, and you still can't see its significance, you're either exhausted, sick, reading something that is terribly written, or are suffering from what I'm talking about, modern disinclination to grapple with written text.

God communicated to mankind finally and utterly in the canon of the Bible; this makes relating to God through the medium of the written word final until Christ returns, and thus Christians must never "grow past" the Word. Christians must ever and always be "people of the Book." To demand something other than the Bible is to dishonor how God has communicated.

But Hebrews 11 does not merely tell us to read the Bible's words; it exhorts us to experience an inner realization or substantiation of its content. We cannot have biblical joy until our eye of faith is keen, until we can really see the things that are invisible. But we cannot change ourselves and make ourselves want to feast our spiritual eye on biblical doctrine. There is no hope in man. Without Christ we can do nothing, especially when it comes to seeing spiritually. So if our eye of faith is myopic, if we are far more inclined to reflect on the things of earth than we are on spiritual realities, if we are distracted, disinclined to read, and dead when we do so, we must cry out with David, "Create in me a clean heart," but this time with a variant: "Create in me a perceptive faith, O God." This is where change starts with everything, fleeing to God in Christ in sorrow for sin, in repentant faith, seeking His Spirit for empowerment.

Without faith we cannot please God or rejoice in Him. And faith is an eye. So set biblical doctrine before your spiritual eye! With God's help you will enjoy a flood of light and joy. As John Flavel wrote, "All other graces, like birds in the nest, depend upon what faith brings in to them; take away faith, and all the graces languish and die: joy, peace, hope, patience, and all the rest depend upon faith."[7]

---

7. Flavel, *Method of Grace*, 132–33.

Study Questions

1. What does "Faith is the substance of things hoped for" mean? What does it not mean? How do you know?

2. How does the immediate context of Hebrews 11 show that faith is an inward faculty of perception? Are there other passages that speak of faith this way? Look through the chapter and find them.

3. How do we exercise our spiritual eye? What can you do to exercise it more?

4. "A key to life is simply taking the time to enjoy biblical truth the way we enjoy a _____."

5. To resist giving attention to biblical doctrine is to resist what? Do you seek to find rest and joy in reflecting on biblical doctrine?

6. What should be the results of reflecting on biblical doctrine?

7. God expects us to avoid distraction, consistently give time to reading the biblical text, and read with a perceptive, substantiating faith that powerfully impacts our soul. Does this describe you? If not, how should you respond to your deadness of heart in order to change?

CHAPTER 10

To Have Joy You Must Obey

Blessed are the pure in heart.

—Matthew 5:8

Acts of obedience themselves are no sign of salvation and are no basis for joy. That may be a startling thing to say at the beginning of a chapter called "To Have Joy You Must Obey." But the Puritans often distinguished between carnal obedience and gospel obedience. Carnal obedience is a fruit of the fallen nature and not a good thing. Gospel obedience is acceptable to God. If you've never considered this, there are few things more important, for the difference is between displeasing and pleasing God, between further sin and evidence of a living faith. The idea that our efforts to serve God could be offensive to Him might come as a bit of a shock.

The Importance of Obedience

Let's talk about the importance of obedience first. Even though acts of obedience can be carnal (and therefore even wrong and, believe it or not, repulsive to God), godly obedience is crucial. It is a vital part of the Christian life; without it the Christian life is a sham. True faith always does good works. The first epistle of John exists in the canon to expand on this point. It presents various ways to test whether a person's faith is living and true. Here are some of these tests: genuine believers do not claim sinlessness (1:8), they confess their sins (v. 9), they love the brothers (2:10–11), they confess Christ (4:2–3), and they listen to the apostles (v. 6). These things are absolute fruits, marks of genuine Christianity, elements of obedience that will be present to some degree or other in anyone who has the Spirit of God.

A multitude of places in Scripture highlight the importance of obeying God. Obedience to God's law is the purpose of regeneration (Ezek. 36:27); therefore, a "Christianity" that downplays the laws of God subverts the goal of the gospel itself and isn't worthy of the name. "Keeping the commandments of God is what matters," Paul said (1 Cor. 7:19). Such obedience, carried out in the Spirit's strength and for God's glory, leads to assurance and thus to joy. Richard Sibbes put it quaintly: "Those that look to be happy must first look to be holy."[1] It is true: to have joy you must obey.

Carnal "Obedience"

As we said before, "obedience" can be evil and not a valid basis for being joyful at all. Consider the Scripture's testimony on this point. Offering a gift to God can be wicked and repulsive to Him: "The sacrifice of the wicked is an abomination; how much more when he brings it with wicked intent!" (Prov. 21:27; cf. Jer. 6:20). The same can be said of prayer: "One who turns away his ear from hearing the law, even his prayer is an abomination" (Prov. 28:9; cf. Isa. 1:15).

False motives spoil otherwise good works. Jesus warned His disciples to avoid this terrible sin that poisons all: "Take heed that you do not do your charitable deeds before men, to be seen by them. Otherwise you have no reward from your Father in heaven" (Matt. 6:1).

External acts of obedience without heart are also evil. "These people draw near to Me with their mouth, and honor Me with their lips, but their heart is far from me" (Matt. 15:8). Praising God with our mouths, an eminently suitable action and one that is commanded, doesn't please God if that praise does not come from the heart. It is just hypocrisy.

Pride ruins obedience too. The Pharisee boasted in prayer, "I fast twice a week; I give tithes of all that I possess" (Luke 18:12). Though God encouraged fasting and commanded tithing, the Pharisee's

---

1. Richard Sibbes, quoted in I. D. E. Thomas, *A Puritan Golden Treasury* (Edinburgh: Banner of Truth, 2007), 158.

obedience was tainted by his self-congratulation and pride. Without humility, acts of obedience are loathsome self-exaltation.

Faith is necessary for obedience to be pleasing: "Without faith it is impossible to please Him" (Heb. 11:6). People in Adam cannot do anything pleasing to God, for their acts are all misdirected away from the glory of God and from gratitude to Him: "The LORD saw that the wickedness of man was great in the earth, and that every intent of the thoughts of his heart was only evil continually" (Gen. 6:5). This passage does not say that every thought of a person's heart is evil but rather every intent, or impulse, of the thoughts. Fallen people misdirect every deed away from its true purpose, that of honoring and esteeming the great and majestic God, and therefore everything an unbeliever does is perverse, even things in the abstract that are good. One interpretation of Proverbs 21:4 makes the point quite memorably: "The plowing of the wicked [is] sin." No matter what they do, even plowing their field, their works are evil, for they do it alienated from God and without the cleansing that comes only from Jesus Christ. Charles Bridges said, "If the fountain-head be bitter, how can the waters be pure?"[2]

The conclusion to be drawn from all this is that acts of obedience are not necessarily godly. Corrupt acts, which may outwardly conform to what God wants to be done, are not obedience at all, for the corrupt vessel from which they come taints them. The Puritans spoke of gospel obedience because they were keenly aware of the many ways fallen nature seeks to congratulate itself by conforming to the current day's view of morality.

It goes without saying that Christians must keep God's commandments—that is, not the commandments they personally like or that a fallen society might be promoting at a given point in time. Christians must obey the commandments God actually gave His people in the Word. And they must do it for the glory of God alone. Many people would agree to this yet their obedience is not gospel obedience at all. Many seem to take obeying God very

---

2. Charles Bridges, *Proverbs* (1846; repr., Edinburgh: Banner of Truth, 1998), 368.

seriously and think of themselves as perfectly capable of doing so without help from Him. Others reject such self-sufficiency yet do not consciously rely on God's Spirit or on Christ's role as mediator, and many others have no concept of union with Christ. Then there are those who obey but not for Christ's sake (Matt. 16:25). The ways to spoil a good work are legion.

It is apparent, then, that gospel obedience is an important idea. In fact, the idea is the way the Puritans distinguished between legalistic obedience (which is man-centered, self-reliant, and not God-honoring) and the obedience of someone who has absorbed the gospel and is relying on it.[3]

To the Puritans it wasn't enough merely to know what legalism is, as if it were only an idea to be studied; they knew it was a mindset, or an approach to life, and they wanted to be able to identify how it manifests itself and how it profoundly yet subtly affects efforts at pleasing God. They knew that it was like leaven and that it leavened the whole lump, turning service to God, which ought to be pure and delightful, into something detestable. In a day in which perverse forms of legalism run rampant, can there be anything more important to understand? It is the difference between wood, hay, and stubble, which will be burned in the fire, and gold, silver, and precious stones, which will glorify God forever.

Gospel Obedience

If you find, to your chagrin, that your obedience has been, to some degree, legalistic, repent and don't despair. The fibers of legalism are often still found in God's saints, and a large part of our Christian lives is to shed these cords and emerge from shackles of coercion into a freer sort of obedience—one that is Christ honoring, freely given, gentle, humble, and, yes, joyful. Fix your eyes on Jesus as you consider the following seven points on what gospel obedience is; several more could undoubtedly be added, but these get to the heart

---

3. An accessible, short study on gospel obedience can be found in Samuel Bolton, *The True Bounds of Christian Freedom* (1645; repr., Edinburgh: Banner of Truth, 2010), 140–44.

of the matter. Taken together they show how gospel obedience leads to joy.

Gospel obedience takes place after conversion. It is impossible to please God without faith in God (Heb. 11:6); therefore, conversion is necessary for obedience to be pleasing to Him. "Obedience" by an unbeliever is displeasing to Him. Gospel obedience is the Spirit-derived sanctification process that comes after God regenerates a person. It is the new nature in action. Without the Spirit, acts of "obedience" are the gesticulations of the fallen nature going through religious motions yet unaware of its own vileness and inability (Eph. 2:1). But when the Spirit renews people, they are purified and are given a new nature, which is characterized as loving God and wanting to serve Him (Deut. 30:6; Ezek. 36:27; 2 Cor. 5:17). The new nature is biased toward God, and that changes the whole tenor of obedience. As William Strong put it, "A man in Christ has his nature changed, and so his pleasures and delights are changed."[4] Conversion takes dislike, fear, coercion, and inability from obedience and adds love, boldness, willingness, and empowerment. Systems of theology that downplay God's sovereign actions in salvation, and which overemphasize man's decisions and works, are predisposed to carnal obedience. Have you trusted the gospel, received the Spirit as the "antidote" to your fallen nature, and obeyed Him gladly out of love? Gospel obedience happens subsequent to, and is predicated on, conversion to Christ and continuing union with Him.

Gospel obedience is carried out with Christ in mind as high priest. Christians are those who "offer up spiritual sacrifices acceptable to God through Jesus Christ" (1 Peter 2:5). Let that verse sink in. Our obedience is to be carried out in the recognition that if we were to obey in our own strength, our efforts would be unacceptable, indeed abominable. Christians ought to offer their acts of obedience to God through Christ. They ought not be thoughtless about good works or think of their works as automatically acceptable to God based on the fact that "I did this good thing." Our works are accepted only

---

4. Strong, *Discourse of the Two Covenants*, 53.

through Him. He lived a righteous life to become our righteousness (1 Cor. 1:30), died on the cross to bear our punishment (Isa. 53:6), and ever lives to intercede for us (Heb. 7:25). Without these priestly ministries of Christ, we would have no hope, for even our obedience after conversion is imperfect and falls far short. Only He is perfect, and we are in Him.

The Old Testament high priest wore a miter, or crown, on his head when he went into the temple to represent the people; the miter had the words "holiness to the Lord" engraved on it, and this symbolized how the high priest sanctified the offerings of the people despite their imperfections and corruptions (Ex. 28:36–38). Obedience that is not carried out with this in mind is implicitly non-Christian, and it isn't humble, for it quietly presumes that the doing of a work is good enough. Just as we pray "in Jesus's name," we should act, think, feel, and live so.

Do you offer your good deeds to God, recognizing their inner faults yet gratefully acknowledging God's grace in the high priesthood of Christ? Do you offer up your obedience as acceptable to God through Christ? Do you consciously say to God, "Lord, I did this good thing, but I know my work is imperfect and sinful, just as I am imperfect and sinful. Accept what I did because of my high priest, Jesus Christ. Thank you that He sanctifies my efforts, as only He can!" This is crucial to living a Christian life, rather than just a moralistic one, and it makes praising God for Jesus Christ a constant aspect of life, for we constantly do things, and if we present the things we do to God through Christ, then Christ has been given His rightful place in our thoughts, as ever present with us, ever needed, and ever relevant.

Gospel obedience is carried out in dependence on union with Christ and on the indwelling Holy Spirit. Jesus said, "Without Me you can do nothing," speaking particularly of our bearing fruit as a branch in a vine, which is a metaphor for our producing good works or obedience (John 15:5). Any obedience therefore must be borne out of conscious need of union with Christ, who gives us the indwelling Holy Spirit, the third person of the Trinity dwelling in our very bodies and providing the inner resources to counteract the flesh (Gal. 5:16). This means we must rely on the Spirit for empowerment. Do you ask God to fill you with His Holy Spirit to empower you and cause you to bear the Spirit's fruit? Doing so is to rely on gospel means, the means that God says we need in order to obey Him. If we think we can obey without His means, we reject His religion for our own, deny the results of the fall, and counter the reasons for Christ's ministry. Exalting self always denigrates Christ. But to engage in gospel obedience is to continually live in light of the great verities of biblical Christianity: we are fallen, weak, and in constant need of God's appointed means of assistance—union with Christ and the indwelling Holy Spirit.

Tragically, relying on Christ and the Spirit can be suppressed by bad preaching. Some preaching is moralistic; that is, it presses the need to obey without consistently pointing listeners to Christ for empowerment. It tacitly presumes human ability. A sin-sick soul who truly fears the ferocity of his fallen nature and has despaired of his own strength will hear little good news from moralistic preachers. Puritan William Strong criticized some of the preachers in his own day: "Men have been pressed to duty without a thorough discovery of man's union with Christ as the ground of his assistance and acceptance." He went on to show the results of this: "And so men have been put upon duties in a moral or legal way, as if they had wrought them by their own strength, and had a power in themselves."[5] Gospel obedience always seeks gospel means. Faith sees what is unseen and believes in union with Christ and the indwelling Spirit, despite these realities being invisible to the physical eye. Do you believe in them, and do you rely on and use them as your only hope in your ongoing fight against sin?

Gospel obedience is done to glorify God out of gratitude for His love. This means that obedience is not carried out in order to gain God's love, or to prove one's worth, or to do good for goodness' sake. All we do is to be done for God's glory (1 Cor. 10:31). Everything

---

5. Strong, *Discourse of the Two Covenants*, 109.

we do is to be done for Christ's sake (Matt. 16:25) and the gospel's (Mark 8:35). This means that gospel obedience does not doubt God's love in Christ but is convinced of it and motivated by it: "The love of Christ compels us" (2 Cor. 5:14). Gospel obedience is an amazed and glad response to the mercies of God in Christ (Rom. 12:1). Without these gospel motives and responses, "obedience" is joyless, selfish, and often full of strife. Is your effort to obey God a grateful response to the gospel and intended to glorify God and not promote yourself?

Gospel obedience delights in God's commandments. "Oh, how I love Your law!" (Ps. 119:97). There is no despising the commandments or loathing the burden of them. The apostle John communicated this quite clearly: "This is the love of God, that we keep His command-ments. And His commandments are not burdensome" (1 John 5:3). John Calvin made some insightful comments on that verse. To sum up his discussion, Calvin said, "'But God's commands are burden-some!' someone protests. 'My reply is that the law is said to be easy if we are endued with heavenly power to overcome our flesh.'"[6] That is gospel obedience! But the ungodly, though they want to be thought good, hate the obligation that commandments place on them. The thought of duty is repugnant to them, and they would get out of it if they could. Gospel obedience, however, delights in the command-ment. Though a sincere Christian won't obey perfectly, he will love the law he wants to obey.

Gospel obedience is carried out with a willing and sincere heart. As William Strong put it, gospel obedience is done with "a free and princely spirit."[7] This is the opposite of a "servile spirit," or an atti-tude that obeys the law but begrudges it as a slave might because he perceives it as coerced and forced on him. A free and princely spirit is obedience that is freely given, as a prince might obey his father the

---

6. John Calvin, *Commentaries*, vol. 22, *1 John* (Grand Rapids: Baker, 1999), 2:252–54. I am indebted to an unpublished statement by Mark Minnick for help on condensing Calvin's comments.

7. For a resource that collects much of what Strong said about "a free and princely spirit," see Thomas Parr, *Backdrop for a Glorious Gospel* (Grand Rapids: Reformation Heritage, 2019), 185n218, 233.

king. Thomas Manton said we obey "as children, not as hirelings!"[8] Gospel obedience is carried out with a volunteer spirit because the heart has been changed and the rebellion removed. As John Flavel explained, "The freedom of obedience is the excellence of it."[9]

You can probably see, upon consideration, that any other sort of obedience would not be accepting of the gospel as it is revealed. Do you accept that God has justified you by faith, though you are ungodly, and that He has placed His love on you regardless of your sins, because of Christ's work? Do you see yourself, sinful as you are, as freed from condemnation (Rom. 8:1) and a child of God, and do you therefore obey without grudging? Is yours a free and princely spirit? Perhaps you have trusted Christ but still have cords of the old nature clinging to you. Rid yourself of them, embrace your condition as God's child, and let that condition permeate all your works to serve Him with freedom.

Gospel obedience is carried out without fear of damnation for remaining sin in our lives. The apostle John wrote that "perfect love casts out fear, because fear involves torment" (1 John 4:18). John may have meant that when we love God perfectly, then we won't avoid Him out of fear of being tormented. Or he may have meant that if we grasp God's perfect love for us, then we won't fear that God will torment us. I think the latter is correct because John said "perfect love," and only God can do that. But either way, he is saying that a proper understanding of God will result in our loving Him, not in our shrinking back from Him. God doesn't want His children to fear damnation. John later says, "These things I have written to you... that you may know that you have eternal life" (1 John 5:13). Are you secure in the truth that God loves you in Christ?

To summarize, obedience that doesn't trust Christ, isn't carried out in reliance on Him as the mediator, isn't carried out in reliance on the empowerment of union with Christ and the indwelling Spirit, isn't convinced of the reality of God's love, and is coerced out of an

8. Thomas Manton, *James* (1693; repr., Edinburgh: Banner of Truth, 1988), 220.
9. Flavel, *Method of Grace*, 108.

unwilling heart is not gospel obedience. But obedience carried out by believers who live their lives with an eye to Christ's mediation, relying on His empowerment through the Spirit, and whose obedience is therefore willing and free, that is a sweet-smelling savor to God in which He delights.

Are We Condemned for Not Fully Obeying in a Gospel Way?

This presentation of gospel obedience shows what sort of obedience is acceptable to God and therefore is a basis for having joy. But it actually may make you feel condemned. Have you realized that you've spent a lot of time "obeying" God without consciously offering up your works to Him through Jesus Christ (1 Peter 2:5)? Have you relied on your own strength rather than the Spirit, not sought the glory of God, or inwardly chafed at God's expectations of you?

Ironically, a message about gospel obedience can feel like condemning law all over again. But the problem is not with the message. Instead of being depressed at your lack of reliance on gospel means or your inability to experience freedom, simply cast yourself on the truth that God receives sinful people in Christ. An old hymn says, "Sing it o'er again, Christ receiveth sinful men!" Fall on your face before God, asking Him to have mercy on you for the vestiges of legalism attached to your life, and take refuge in Christ your mediator. He makes up for your lack, all your sin, even your faulty obedience! It is why He came into this world (1 Tim. 2:5; Col. 2:13). Then keep hold of that reliance on Christ throughout your life. Obey hand in hand with Christ and with a believing, humble, and free spirit rather than with an independent, proud, and servile spirit. Start living with the joy of gospel obedience. Fully trust Jesus to deal with all your failings and deficiencies and to make up for all the imperfections in your service to God, which are legion. Ultimately, gospel obedience is carried out by people who are fully aware of their wretched sinfulness and have their eyes firmly fixed, joyously, on Jesus. May this life of gospel obedience be your experience. It is truly a basis for joy, for it is built directly on the foundation of Jesus Christ (Col. 2:6–7).

Study Questions

1. What is the difference between carnal obedience and gospel obedience?

2. What did Richard Sibbes mean when he said, "Those that look to be happy must first look to be holy."

3. How do we know that acts of "obedience" can be sinful? What Scriptures show us that they can be?

4. What things make a "good work" repulsive to God?

5. How did the Puritans respond to knowing that legalism is a mindset, or an approach to life?

6. Why are acts of obedience undertaken before conversion unacceptable to God?

7. Why should acts of obedience be offered consciously to God through Christ?

8. Why should obedience be undertaken with conscious dependence on the Spirit?

9. How can bad preaching take people off gospel means?

10. Is your obedience carried out in gratitude for God's assured love in Christ without resentment toward His commands?

11. What do you do if you discover that your obedience has been legalistic to a certain degree? Is "gospel obedience" a new law to which you must measure up?

CHAPTER 11

Joy in an Incomprehensible God

The secret things belong to the LORD our God, but those things which are revealed belong to us and to our children forever, that we may do all the words of this law.
—Deuteronomy 29:29

Scripture contains some enigmas that are solvable puzzles but others that are unanswerable mysteries. Many hard things in the Bible are like mountain peaks that take work to climb, but they provide a wonderful view once you ascend to the top. But some mysteries in the Bible can never be fully understood. These mountaintops are scalable to a degree but are always wreathed in a dazzling cloud that astounds the perceptions of mere humans. Once you've done your best, you still can't get a perfectly clear view.

Consider the doctrine of the Trinity. When you really grapple with what the Bible says about God, you begin to encounter statements that need reconciling. God is one God (Deut. 6), yet the Word, who is in fact God, was "in the beginning with God" (see John 1:1–3). The Word *is* God and was *with* God at the same time. Taken together, these verses from Deuteronomy and John point out the singularity of God while also specifying the plurality of persons in the Trinity. But understanding the basic concept does not mean it is completely comprehensible. There is no problem with the doctrine; the issue is that mankind cannot fully grasp the infinite God.

Sometimes truth about God "is too wonderful for me; it is high, I cannot attain it" (Ps. 139:6). This doesn't mean that God is self-contradictory, confused, or unable to communicate in a clear way.

Nor does it imply any defect in God. It means that God is incomprehensible. He is infinite and we are finite, and therefore we cannot ever hope to have exhaustive knowledge of Him. We should expect to run into unsolvable mysteries when reflecting on Him.

God's incomprehensibility is not a manmade idea but is taught in the Bible. Paul prays that believers would "know the love of Christ which passes knowledge" (Eph. 3:19). The psalmist said, "Great is the LORD…and His greatness is unsearchable" (Ps. 145:3). God has revealed things about Himself that we can know, but ultimately His greatness is too great to be fully grasped by finite man.

Many people find these thoughts insulting and insist that we ought to be able to fully grasp anything that God teaches. Others find them alienating—you can't love God if you can't comprehend Him. Some might even feel that God's incomprehensibility makes Him suspect; it opens up the possibility that we might discover negative "surprises" about Him, sort of like a woman who marries a man without knowing him and wakes up one day realizing she's married a monster. Obviously these responses rule out joy. You can't rejoice in God if you feel insulted by Him, alienated from Him, or suspicious of Him. To some, the doctrine of God's incomprehensibility is a dark place they'd rather avoid.

Why God's Incomprehensibility Should Fuel Joy

God's incomprehensibility is actually a great blessing and ought to fuel our joy. Let's consider four reasons why.

First, God's incomprehensibility tells us God is worthy of worship. If we could figure Him out, He wouldn't be God. If we could master Him, He wouldn't be the high and lofty God who is above all the nations and above the heavens (Ps. 113). God's incomprehensibility gives us a concrete way to glorify Him. Paul does this exact thing: "Oh, the depth of the riches both of the wisdom and knowledge of God! How unsearchable are His judgments and His ways past finding out!… To whom be glory forever" (Rom. 11:33, 36).

Far from making us feel alienated or suspicious, God's inscrutable ways should lead us to awe and doxology. How could we take joy in a god who is small enough to be fully comprehended by man? We couldn't. The true God, the only God worthy of worship, must be beyond us. As Augustine wrote, "We are speaking of God. Is it any wonder if you do not comprehend? For if you comprehend, it is not God you comprehend. Let it be a pious confession of ignorance rather than a rash profession of knowledge. To attain some slight knowledge of God is a great blessing; to comprehend him, however, is totally impossible."[1]

Second, the doctrine shows us our smallness and reminds us we are finite. David reflected on the heavens as the work of God's fingers and asked, "What is man?" We range only among the outskirts of His ways. We are small and vulnerable and must cling to our great God in childlike faith. When we see ourselves as small before the majesty of God, we reach out to Him in the realization of what we are (needy), and by reaching out to Him, we confess He is sufficient. We become dependent rather than suspicious.

Third, the doctrine leads us to cling to what He has revealed about Himself in the Word. Instead of allowing incomprehensibility to cause us to distrust God, we should be grateful for what we do in fact know of Him. The revealed things tell us that God is merciful and gracious to sinners, even to the point of suffering for their redemption. Yes, we do walk through some enigmatic places, but the hand that holds ours as we walk through those places is nail-scarred. The great mysterious God is no ogre but is revealed in Scripture to be our Loving Shepherd who lays down His life for the sheep. Knowing what is revealed takes the fear out of what is hidden. Being aware of hidden things makes us rely on what is revealed.

Fourth, God's incomprehensibility helps us see Him as an endless source of fresh blessing; we have an eternal, satisfying source of beauty and object of praise before us. God is infinite, so we'll never come to the end of Him. We'll never know Him exhaustively. A person might misunderstand the statement "I shall know just as I also

---

1. Augustine, quoted in Herman Bavinck, *Reformed Dogmatics* (Grand Rapids: Baker, 2009), 2:48.

am known" in 1 Corinthians 13:12. This statement does not refer
to knowing God comprehensively as God knows us, for that would
demand that we become omniscient. It means we will know God
in the fullest way a glorified human can know Him. In time and
eternity, we will forever be learning more and more from a fountain
of truth and life and beauty that will never run dry. That is a joyful
thing, and it is clear that this doctrine is no dark place.

Misconstruals of the Doctrine

It is important to bring up some things that the doctrine of God's
incomprehensibility does not imply. There are plenty of ways to go
astray here, and these errors may contribute to people's distress at
this doctrine. Consider these cautions: the doctrine doesn't imply
that God is unknowable; or that our knowledge, being incomplete,
is therefore not reliable; or that the more we know the less we know;
or that we can't know God's essence; or that we must always dither
about in a fog of puzzlement and uncertainty.

These misconstruals all share one major error—they imply
that seeking to know God is a waste of time. In fact, you can detect
uncareful statements of this doctrine when they seem agnostic, as
if we can't know God or we will always be in the dark about Him.
It appears to be very easy to take this glorious doctrine of God's
incomprehensibility and (unwittingly) use it to denigrate God, His
revelation, and His knowability.

I've sometimes heard theologians say that when we speak of
God, we're babbling like infants or are being spoken to by God in
"baby talk." I understand that these theologians are simply trying to
help people see the profound distinction between God and man, and
in so doing they are right, but such illustrations verge on belittling
our knowledge of God and perhaps even verging into the territory of
agnosticism. Scripture itself speaks of our knowledge of the infinite
God quite differently: "My mouth shall tell of Your righteousness and Your salvation all the day, for I do not know their limits"
(Ps. 71:15). The logic of this verse is that the psalmist's inability
to fully know God led him to continually speak about Him. The

illimitable amount of knowledge leads him to feel the need to constantly speak of God's righteousness and salvation. The verse honors the task of knowing and telling of God, based on the greatness of the God who is known. We must not denigrate the knowledge of God or make it seem poor and pitiable. To belittle our knowledge of God is to belittle the God we know.

Nevertheless, it is true that God is beyond us and has graciously stooped not merely to behold man but also to communicate with him (Ps. 113:6). His knowledge is different from ours, though analogous, and we cannot know Him comprehensively. But our knowledge of Him is true if it conforms to His Word, and that knowledge must be spoken of in respectful terms, for it is knowledge of God.

Our Joyful Response

Now let's see how knowledge of God's incomprehensibility ought to affect our lives in very significant ways. Consider three points: the doctrine should inspire awe and wonder, motivate contentment and satisfaction, and promote humble gratitude.

First, knowing the infinite God should inspire awe and wonder. When people grasp incomprehensibility, they begin to view themselves as explorers on the shining borders of eternity. They are surrounded by wonders that challenge description, marvels they can grapple with and indeed understand and explain but rarely to their own satisfaction. They realize that once they enter the next life, things become more wondrous forever, and they will spend eternity traveling with their Savior "further up and further in" (as C. S. Lewis put it in *The Last Battle*) toward and through the endless glory of God. Eternity will be all about grasping more and more, truly and accurately, yet never coming to an end of knowledge, seeing and yet always finding more glory and splendor. How could it be otherwise, given that we will be knowing the infinite God?

Second, knowing the infinite God should motivate contentment and satisfaction. Nothing gives a sense of safety and contentment more than knowing you have a well-stocked larder filled with the best foodstuffs for the long winter months ahead. Repleteness gives you a sense of cheerful satisfaction, the opposite of the unsettled fear of a shortage. God's incomprehensibility inspires joy, for we can always expect to find more in God. He is a never-ending source of pleasure, interest, beauty, health, and life. Such contentment admits people's inherent hunger and need but exults in God's abundant supply to meet those needs. We ought to relish the prospect of knowing the all-sufficient God more and more throughout life and eternity. Hear the same longing and relish in the psalmist's words: "One thing I have desired of the LORD...that I may dwell in the house of the LORD all the days of my life, to behold the beauty of the LORD" (Ps. 27:4).

Finally, it should promote humble gratitude. When we see God's greatness and incomprehensibility, we'll never proudly say, "I don't need to listen to any more sermons or read the Bible any more. I've got this God stuff down." When we grasp His profundity, our eyes will be opened and our smallness will come crashing home, but so will His bigness. We will realize God cannot be shelved like a college course one has mastered. Any idea that we can master Him reveals our ignorance. Humility will come, and our pursuit of Him will be marked by a sense of massive privilege. We will see that our place, that of gazing and glorying at the effulgence of glory that is in God, is a blessing that should elicit constant gratitude and never tedium.

Ultimately God's incomprehensibility is described from the perspective of God's infinite nature and man's finite mind. God is mind-blowing, and you cannot comprehend Him, yet He is your Savior who has committed Himself in all His greatness to loving you forever. Some things are above humanity's pay grade, but there is a joy and comfort in leaving difficult matters with your Savior, who is mercifully beyond you but who died for you and can be trusted with mysterious things.

Study Questions

1. Where is the doctrine of God's incomprehensibility taught in the Bible?

2. What are some wrong responses to this doctrine? Why might some people consider it a dark thing?

3. What are four reasons God's incomprehensibility should fuel joy?

4. What are some misconstruals of the doctrine?

5. What is the common denominator among all the misconstruals?

6. In what sense is it true that we speak in "baby talk" when we speak of God? In what sense is it not true? Why is it important to be careful talking about our knowledge this way?

7. This doctrine fuels joy in what three ways? Why should it fuel joy in these ways?

CHAPTER 12

Joy and Problem People
in the Church

Our light affliction, which is but for a moment, is working for us
a far more exceeding and eternal weight of glory, while we do not
look at the things which are seen, but at the things which are not
seen. For the things which are seen are temporary, but the things
which are not seen are eternal.
                                                    —2 Corinthians 4:17–18

Aside from Christ Himself, if anyone exemplifies maintaining joy despite problem people, it is the apostle Paul. He rejoiced consistently, even when at the hands of unbelievers he was beaten, stoned, imprisoned, and ultimately martyred. Professing Christians mistreated him too. It is shocking (or it should be) to behold all the ways he was mistreated by people who were associated with the Christian church.

Paul Mistreated by Professing Christians

Paul was belittled by professing Christians. Antagonists at Corinth, for example, didn't think much of him: "'His letters,' they say, 'are weighty and powerful, but his bodily presence is weak, and his speech contemptible'" (2 Cor. 10:10). Rather than humbly listening to Paul's teaching, they indulged their inner faultfinder. They wouldn't sit under the preaching because they were too busy sitting over the preacher.

Paul was slandered by professing Christians. His opponents in Corinth spoke of Paul as robbing other churches by accepting support from them (2 Cor. 11:8). They cast aspersions on him, calling him a thief. You may wonder if they were really being serious, but even if they weren't, Paul speaks of having to endure slander as a matter of course (6:8). Slander was common, and unfortunately it still is, undoubtedly because the devil, whose very name means "the slanderous one," is quite busy inspiring similar activities in people (Eph. 2:2).

Paul was abused by professing Christians. When he was in prison for Christ, some people preached the gospel in order to make things worse for him there. Paul said they "preach Christ from selfish ambition, not sincerely, supposing to add affliction to my chains" (Phil. 1:16). It boggles the mind that people who evidently cared about preaching the message of Christ (v. 18) could treat His apostle this way.

Finally, Paul was abandoned by his Christian friends at an especially painful moment. On one occasion, probably when the emperor Nero was blaming Christians for the burning of Rome, Paul had to defend his actions: "At my first defense no one stood with me, but all forsook me. May it not be charged against them" (2 Tim. 4:16). The apostle, who gave so much to people, lost all human companionship when facing one of his greatest trials. This fact is almost as stunning as Paul's gracious prayer for them to be forgiven.

It sounds like the Christian community was quite awful! Tragically, the institutional church has always been a mixed multitude. It has wolves in sheep's clothing in it. It also contains many genuine but vacillating Christians—people who choose to follow the world and the flesh, often for years. Sometimes it is hard to tell the difference between wolves and broken sheep. The church invisible is gloriously triumphant, but the visible church often presents a dramatically different picture. A person must have faith in invisible things in order to stay encouraged.

Many people do not stay encouraged. They abandon the church because they are disillusioned by others. About a decade ago a well-known person left an organized Christian denomination, saying in essence, "I still love Christ, but I cannot be associated with this deservedly notorious group of people." That is a scathing remark. Though I do not know the details of the situation, I suspect the person's response was unjust. But even if there are complicating factors, it does not follow that there are no extreme sinners in the church that defame it. When I went into Christian ministry fifteen years ago, a relative of mine told me with genuine concern, "Watch out for those church people; they will stab you in the back, suck you dry, and chew you up." It was memorable to hear someone say that. At the time, I remember being shocked. Another family member, who knew nothing about the words of the first person, said, "I wish you would reconsider becoming a pastor, because church people kick you in the teeth." I specifically remember the phrase "kick you in the teeth." Apparently, these are common sentiments. I can drive down many streets in my town and see the houses of people who have told me they've been "burnt" by "mean people" and therefore won't go back to any church at all. Surely some of these incidents were, truth be told, misunderstandings or exaggerations. Yet we would be naive to presume that the church doesn't contain harmful people in it. It clearly does (see Acts 20:29–30; 1 Cor. 3:1–3; 2 Tim. 4:3; Jude 4).

How do we respond to this dark place? We cannot neglect Christian fellowship as so many do (Heb. 10:25). We also must not attend church while expecting everyone around us to fail or, even worse, while "holding our nose" at those around us. Abandoning church or being self-righteous turns us into the problem people we object to. What are we to do? How are we to cope with this common problem?

A marvelous thing about Paul is that he joyfully kept serving the church despite problem people. One wonders about the secret of his joy. How did Paul show God's amazing grace toward problem people in the church? Five points from 2 Corinthians and Philippians will show us a lot about how Paul remained joyful and faithful even in the face of this dark thing that discourages so many of us. Since these points are drawn from Paul, they especially relate to those in Christian leadership (particularly point 3), but most of them can be applied by any believer.

How Paul Kept Serving despite Problem People in the Church

Paul endured joyfully because he *put Christ's interests over his own.*
He rejoiced even when people preached the gospel to increase his
misery. "Whether in pretense or in truth, Christ is preached; and
in this I rejoice, yes, and will rejoice" (Phil. 1:18). No doubt it would
have been tempting for Paul to become bitter at how he was being
treated. But by God's grace he invested himself in the cause of Christ,
whether or not he was laid aside or persecuted. He cared more about
Christ's advancement than his own comfort (Acts 20:24).

Putting self first can be subtle, but its effects are profound, for
when injustices come, all sorts of fleshly responses result: bitterness,
protests, outbursts, depression. Putting Christ first, as Paul did, is
vital to maintaining joy despite problem people. "It doesn't matter
what happens to me. Only that Christ's cause prospers!" When you
put Christ's interests first, personal harm becomes endurable. You
may worry that Christ's cause will suffer if you are insulted or slandered, but you must trust the Lord's commitment to His own name
and to your ultimate good. John Flavel remarked that "as for your
innocency, God will clear it up."[1]

Paul endured joyfully because he *had the perception to see God at
work in the world* (2 Cor. 7:4–16). In 2 Corinthians 7, Paul says that
he was very downcast about their state (v. 5), but God encouraged
him by the arrival of Titus, who told him about their godly response
to Paul's last letter (vv. 6–7). They got things right rather than object-
ing to Paul the way his detractors did (vv. 8–11). Throughout the
book, Paul ascribes their right response to God. He says it was God
who comforted him with the news of their response; God "comforts
the downcast" (v. 6).

Any time Christians exhibited virtues like faith, repentance, and
love, Paul gave credit to Christ (e.g., Phil. 1:6; 2:13; 1 Cor. 15:10). He
saw godly behavior for what it is—the work of the Spirit, bringing
purity out of a corrupt one born in Adam. He saw people's godliness

---

1. Flavel, *Fountain of Life*, 293.

as evidence that God had indeed saved them, for a changed life happens only by God's grace. Without Christ we can do nothing (John 15:5). This means Paul saw God at work anytime a Christian bore fruit.

Perceiving God at work is crucial to having joy. Paul snatched joy out of the jaws of sorrow; he was "sorrowful, yet always rejoicing" (2 Cor. 6:10). Paul was constantly overcoming discouragement by faith, constantly dispelling darkness with God's light. One way he did that was by perceiving God at work. We too must see light in a Christian as the work of God. Too often we grumble over imperfections. Whenever we find true Christian virtue in this sin-cursed world, we should mark the grace of God and rejoice.

Paul endured joyfully because he *refused to be judged by carnal people but trusted God's call*. Paul said, "We dare not class ourselves or compare ourselves with those who commend themselves. But they, measuring themselves by themselves, and comparing themselves among themselves, are not wise" (2 Cor. 10:12).

When Paul said he did not dare to enter into such a comparison, he was not afraid of coming through it looking unfavorable. He was saying that he refused to allow man to validate him as a worthy minister. Paul's confidence rested "within the limits of the sphere which God appointed" him (2 Cor. 10:13). He trusted God was wise when He called Paul to serve. People's purported right to bequeath approval is unimportant. He says, "It is a very small thing that I should be judged by you" (1 Cor. 4:3).

This sense of calling led Paul to joyfully depend on God's wisdom, not on personal traits people take pride in. Paul depended on the Lord to make him, a mere clay pot, sufficient to carry out ministry (see 2 Cor. 3:5; 4:7). He did not rely on charm, oratorical expertise, a strong stage presence, a fine pulpit voice, style, administrative skill, or any other quality that carnal people want to enshrine as a minister's qualifying characteristic.

Though this point applies most directly to ministers, it has relevance to any Christian who wants to serve God. There is joy in confessing inherent unworthiness and inability and not feeling the need to justify one's worth before the tribunal of self-righteous people. There is peace in relying on God's sufficiency rather than one's supposed personal greatness. Everything we have, including any personal talent, is from God, so we must not boast as if it were somehow our own doing (1 Cor. 4:7).

Paul was handpicked by Christ on the Damascus road, so he had a profound sense of call, but ministers today should have it too. If a pastor is not self-anointed, then he can point to many evidences of God's providential call on his life—various churches' testimonies to his giftedness, other pastors' approval, his seminary professors' testimony, his ordination council's approval, not to mention the many encouraging words from individuals who have been helped by his ministry. It is crucial that ministers have these varied and independent witnesses, for together they commend him to a flock and provide him a sense of divine calling. Times will come when critics strike, sometimes harshly and even en masse, and if the man of God is insecure in His call, he will be shaken, lose joy, and perhaps abandon the ministry God gave him.

Paul endured joyfully because he *saw people's insults as an opportunity to rely on Christ's strength.* "I will rather boast in my infirmities, that the power of Christ may rest upon me. Therefore I take pleasure...in reproaches" (2 Cor. 12:9–10). Note in these verses that Paul includes "reproaches," or insults, among the infirmities in which he boasts. When people insulted Paul, he took pleasure in the opportunity to manifest God's power: "When I am weak, then I am strong" (v. 10). But if you lean on the arm of the flesh, insults will expose your vain confidence, for you will protest, justify self, or revile those who revile you. You want to be appreciated or respected, so when the opposite occurs, you respond sinfully. But operating in the power of the Spirit says, "I am indeed weak, a mere clay pot, but Christ's strength is with the weak who look to Him!" The Spirit brings this choice wine from your life the more you are squeezed by hardship.

It should go without saying that insults are different from brotherly rebukes for sin. Godly people admit faults and seek to grow in godliness, and they graciously weigh even inept attempts at giving advice. We should all be very slow to view input as reproach. It is a subtle form of pride to call bungling but good-faith attempts at constructive criticism "persecution." Doing so insulates ourselves from advice and all but guarantees we will never learn to understand other people's perspectives. Yes, much advice is poorly thought-out, poorly worded, and perhaps even sinful, but there is usually something useful to be gleaned from it. A humble person will find the gold nugget among the refuse and thank even unstable people for their efforts to help.

Paul viewed insults as opportunities to rely on Christ's power. He admitted his weakness but gloried in God's strength given to those who abandon pride and humbly seek the Lord. When people stoop to cruelty and insults, there is a joy in replying, "My insufficiency leads me to trust God's all-sufficiency."

Paul endured joyfully because he *looked at the things that are unseen.* He speaks of being "hard-pressed," or under high pressure (2 Cor. 4:8). He says he was "persecuted" and "struck down," both physically and emotionally (v. 9). But Paul's method for remaining joyful and steadfast in these trials, finding new strength every day (v. 16), was to keep his eye on invisible and eternal things (v. 18). This means he kept his mind on God, Christ, salvation, and heaven.

Paul spends so much time in Ephesians speaking of God's eternal redemptive plans in Christ. Paul wrote Ephesians to help believers who had found out about his imprisonment and were tempted to be discouraged by his trials (Eph. 3:13). He expounds all that the Father has done, is doing, and will do in Christ for the church to the praise of His glory (1:3–14). He keeps using the phrase "in the heavenly places" because he is lifting our gaze to heaven. Paul and his readers needed the encouragement of invisible and eternal things—things only the eye of faith can see.

You are going to face discouragement, probably even from other believers. You will be tempted to lose yourself in entertainment, hobbies, relationships, and activities. But Paul coped by gazing at eternal, invisible things. We too must fix our eye of faith where Christ sits. Read the New Testament looking for all things heavenly, invisible, eternal. When you find passages that dwell on invisible things, meditate on them, turning them into heartfelt prayers, expressions of longing, and praises. Repent of not wanting to do this, and ask God to change your heart by His Spirit until you are made willing. Read good Christian literature that contains deep reflections on things that are invisible.[2] Make friends with heavenly minded people and speak with them often about God.

Forgive as God Has Forgiven You

Upon further reflection, there is a sixth element that should be added to this discussion, and it has the benefit of keeping you from applying any of the above truths in pride. When people abuse you, you must forgive them based on God's forgiving you. Jesus taught this truth in Matthew 18:23–35, and Paul clearly had grasped it. He says that "a servant of the Lord must not quarrel but be gentle to all, able to teach, patient, in humility correcting those who are in opposition" (2 Tim. 2:24–25). The word *patient* in this text means to patiently endure evil treatment without recrimination of heart or action.

Even the most confrontational aspect of ministry, rebuking, is to be done with longsuffering (2 Tim. 4:2). But how can you be patient and longsuffering toward those who mistreat you? You do it by keeping in mind how patient God has been with you. Paul says, "Christ Jesus came into the world to save sinners, of whom I am chief. However, for this reason I obtained mercy, that in me first Jesus Christ might show all longsuffering, as a pattern to those who are going to believe on Him" (1 Tim. 1:15–16).

Paul was patient with sinners because he was aware of how God had shown patience to him. This response is short-circuited when we do not feel sinful, for then we stop marveling at God's forgiveness. Paul said he is the chief of sinners, and he did so late in his life! This sense of your own unworthiness reminds you not to view other

---

2. Some examples are Augustine's *Confessions*, John Bunyan's *Pilgrim's Progress*, John Flavel's *Fountain of Life*, and Samuel Rutherford's *Letters*.

people's sin from a lofty vantage. Remembering your own sin—and God's amazing grace to you despite it—prompts you to lump yourself in with other sinners rather than exalt yourself over them.

You are (or should be) "poor in spirit," realizing you are a spiritual beggar among other beggars, a man of unclean lips among a people of unclean lips (see Isa. 6:5). When you see others sin, even when they sin against you, you have a basis for humility and compassion. Any scorn or recrimination, coming from a wretch like you, would be unjust and hypocritical. As you serve others, always remember that you are just a beggar showing other beggars where you have found bread—in Jesus Christ, the bread of life.

Study Questions

1. In what four ways was Paul mistreated by professing Christians?

2. Which Scripture passages show that the visible church is a mixed multitude—that is, made up of saved and unsaved people, even some who cause harm?

3. What are some wrong reactions to the presence of problem people in the church?

4. What are the five points that show how Paul endured joyfully despite problem people in the church?

5. What passages show that God deserves the glory for a Christian's godly behavior?

6. When you face situations that point out your insufficiency, what trait is God developing in you?

7. What are some things you can do to keep your eye fixed on invisible things?

8. Why is a sense of unworthiness crucial to being able to forgive others and show patience?

9. How does Matthew 18:23–35 help keep a person humble? How does the magnitude of your sin against God encourage your forgiving others? Read the passage and answer.

CHAPTER 13

Joy in Old Testament Promises to Israel

All the promises of God in Him are Yes.
—2 Corinthians 1:20

As you read your Old Testament, you'll reach the Hebrew prophets—Isaiah, Jeremiah, Ezekiel, and the others. Many of these books are filled with judgments but also with wonderful promises. As you read through them, it is a relief to encounter the promises because they are rays of light in very dark contexts filled with doom. But their refreshing light can be dispelled if we think, "Perhaps this was just for Israel. Should I take it as God speaking to me or not?"

Are You Excluded?

You shouldn't relish an expression of love if it was never meant for you. It would be like listening over the fence and overhearing someone declaring their affection to their lover and taking it as though it were spoken to you. You hear the tender words and burst through the fence, saying, "Oh, thank you; I love you too." You'd never be welcome at their house again.

To many Christians the Bible, particularly the Old Testament, seems to have been written to people who were in a very different relationship with God. These Christians feel alienated from God when they read it. This is a tragic mistake that makes the Bible perhaps not a dark place but a shadowy one.

Here is an example of what I am talking about. Imagine yourself up early, and you've got a steaming cup and an open Bible in front of you. You need God, and you feel it. The dark things in the world are wearying as usual, so you are seeking green pastures in Scripture. You encounter these exquisite words:

> Sing, O heavens!
> Be joyful, O earth!
> And break out in singing, O mountains!
> For the LORD has comforted His people,
> And will have mercy on His afflicted.

> But Zion said, "The LORD has forsaken me,
> And my LORD has forgotten me."

> "Can a woman forget her nursing child,
> And not have compassion on the son of her womb?
> Surely they may forget,
> Yet I will not forget you.
> See, I have inscribed you on the palms of My hands;
> Your walls are continually before Me." (Isa. 49:13–16)

You personalize the passage as you should; God is encouraging you to sing joyfully, to trust His compassion. God describes His love to you—He is more devoted than a nursing mother and has engraved you on the palms of His hands. You think, "It doesn't get much better than this!" You feel like God is your father in a very real way. But then you read the final statement: "Your walls are continually before me." Images of fortifications spring up in your mind's eye, and you picture the ancient Middle Eastern city of Jerusalem, which is undoubtedly what Isaiah had in mind. You stop personalizing the passage and think, "Oh, He's talking to Israel, not to me."

Have you ever had an experience like this? Delight turns to doubt as you begin to suspect you've been listening over that fence. What do you do? Should you walk away from the passage feeling excluded, like a distant acquaintance or, worse, a bystander? Not on your life. If you are to experience joy from your Bible reading, you must see how every promise relates to Christ, your Lord and Shepherd, and thus to you. Of course there is always the danger of assuming illegitimate parallels, such as viewing every event in the life of Jacob as prefiguring Christ. But in this chapter I am more concerned with another danger, that of feeling as if the Old Testament was for Israel, not the church, and therefore being suspicious of parallels and feeling alienated from the Old Testament. Below are some fundamental points that will help you sort through such experiences and maintain joyful relationship with God when you read the Old Testament.

Not a Bystander

First, the Old Testament was not written solely to the people who lived in those times but to New Testament believers also. Peter says, "not to themselves, but to us they [the prophets] were ministering" (1 Peter 1:12). He insists that the Old Testament was written to New Testament believers. If this is hard to swallow, just listen to Paul: "Whatever things were written before were written for our learning, that we through the patience and comfort of the Scriptures might have hope" (Rom. 15:4); "All these things…were written for our admonition" (1 Cor. 10:11). Peter and Paul are both telling us that the Old Testament was written to Christians. If you have true faith in Christ, the Old Testament was written to you; you are the intended audience.

The Old Testament can even bring people to a saving knowledge of Christ. Paul tells Timothy that "from childhood you have known the Holy Scriptures, which are able to make you wise for salvation through faith which is in Christ Jesus" (2 Tim. 3:15). This is not true only since the New Testament has come, for Abraham and Moses both were believers in Christ (John 8:56; Heb. 11:26), and Anna and Simeon were Old Testament believers who knew of Christ and were anticipating His coming (Luke 2:25–26, 36–38). Jesus described the Old Testament Scriptures as "they which testify of Me" (John 5:39). The Old Testament is Christian.

That feeling of being excluded that I mentioned earlier must be discarded in light of apostolic teaching. Theologians may debate the specifics of how Old Testament promises relate to us, but ultimately, if you are a believer, God does not want you to feel like those precious promises are for someone else and not for you. When you read

the Law, the Prophets, and the Writings, you are not listening over
the fence to someone else's conversation.

For example, when God says to Israel, "I have loved you with
an everlasting love" (Jer. 31:3), He is speaking to the elect in Israel
thousands of years ago, but since you are an elect child of Abraham
by faith in Christ (Gal. 3:7, 29; Rom 2:28–29), it applies to you. You
should feel confident about interpreting such expressions as referring directly to you. The reference to Jerusalem's walls in Isaiah 49:16
can't negate the reality that God has written you on the palm of His
hand, which is a striking metaphor for being unalterably present
with you in a special way that makes Him keenly aware of you. Imagine how many times a day you would see engravings on your palms.
God has bound you to Himself in such a way that He is always seeing
you. That promise is yours to rejoice in.

Second, the Old Testament was written to preach Christ. Sometimes people get the notion that the Old Testament was all about
land, war, and politics, while the New Testament introduces salvation, heaven, Christ, and the church. But this reflects a superficial
reading of the Old Testament. It is more focused on national matters
than the New Testament is, but from the very beginning it is about
faith in Christ and has heaven in view.[1] Paul understood that God's
plans about Christ are eternal (Eph. 3:11). The New Testament is not
the result of God "shifting gears" or reshaping the Bible's message;
it is the result of God fulfilling His purposes. We should therefore
expect the message about Christ to be found in the Old Testament. It
includes hundreds of direct predictions of Him or statements about

---

1. For just a small sampling, take a look at Genesis 3:15; 5:24; 15:6; Psalm 2:12;
23:6 in their contexts. Genesis 3:15 gives the Bible's first glimpse of the coming suffering savior, while 5:24 shows a believing individual being delivered from death
and taken to a place beyond earth. Genesis 15:6 explains that Abraham was justified
by faith, and Psalm 2:12 encourages faith to be placed in the Son of God. Psalm 23:6
shows a believer looking forward to dwelling in God's house forever, a clear reference to life after death in heaven with God. Taken together, these five verses show
that people are saved from death and gain eternal life in heaven by trusting in the
Son of God. The idea that the Old Testament is all about earthly concerns and the
New Testament is heavenly is clearly an error.

Him as well as types, institutional symbols, and the sacrificial system, which prefigured Him. Seeing these things will invite you to find your Savior in the Old Testament, and your feeling of alienation will be gone.

Third, the Old Testament gospel is your gospel. The Old Testament does not promote a different way of salvation than the New Testament. Thinking that it does can make you feel alienated from your Bible, as if it were written to people who were in a fundamentally different relationship to God than you are. It is vital to see ourselves as part of the same "tree" as believers in the Old Testament, just as Paul explains in Romans 11:17 and Ephesians 2:12–13. In fact, Paul tells us that believers in the Old Testament believed the same gospel we do. He says the gospel was preached to Abraham (Gal. 3:8), and the writer of Hebrews concurs; the gospel was preached to the nation of Israel (Heb. 4:2). We may think of Old Testament saints as only law-focused, herding flocks, fighting wars. But in the midst of their very earthy lives, they had a messianic hope (Gen. 49:10, 18). It was all their desire (2 Sam. 23:5). Old Testament people were encouraged to trust Christ (see Ps. 2:12), and some did (Heb. 11:26). In short, the Old Testament gospel was and is our gospel, and Old Testament saints were believers in Christ like us.

Fourth, believers in Christ are and always have been God's chosen people. Paul points out that God chose Jacob rather than Esau, though both were natural sons of Isaac and Rebekah and of the same ethnic stock (Rom. 9:13). Therefore, ethnicity has nothing to do with being chosen, or elect, and it never has. Paul speaks of his own ethnicity as having absolutely no value in relation to being right with God (Phil. 3:5, 7). He says its value in making him right with God can be compared to that of rubbish or dung. That's strong language, and Paul must have felt it necessary to say it that way because people have tended to think of themselves as being right with God due to their relations. Paul says the true Jew is anyone who has a circumcised heart (Rom. 2:28–29; Phil. 3:3).

Someone might wonder, "If Jewish ethnicity is so unimportant, why does the Old Testament focus on Israel as God's chosen people?" There are actually many reasons that God focused on Israel in the Old Testament, but the most important is that He intended to bring Christ from the seed of Abraham to bless all the families of the earth (Gen. 12:3). God did not focus on Israel because He is biased toward a special race of people (after all, all people have sinned and deserve God's wrath) but because salvation was going to come from the Jews—that is, through the Jewish messiah: "salvation is of the Jews" (John 4:22). Therefore, God's Jew-centeredness in the Old Testament was really a focus on all peoples. Again, it is important to recognize that believers in Christ are God's chosen people: "You are a chosen generation, a royal priesthood, a holy nation, His own special people...who once were not a people but are now the people of God" (1 Peter 2:9–10).

If you are reading about how God promises Israel that its number will "be as the sand of the sea" (Hos. 1:10; cf. Gen. 32:12), don't feel excluded from that promise as if it referred only to ethnic Israel. This promise clearly had an Old Testament fulfillment in the multiplication of the Jewish nation, but it has an even greater fulfillment in Christians, who are true Jews (Rom. 2:28–29), who are of every kindred and tribe, and who are also Abraham's children (Gal. 3:29). To put it most simply, if you're a believer, you are part of the family. Believers in Christ are God's chosen people. You should see yourself in the expressions of grace to Israel in the Old Testament. Yes, there will be nuance at times as to how to apply Old Testament verses to yourself, but you should be inclined to apply them, not feel excluded from them.

Finally, remember that all God's promises are affirmed in Christ. "All the promises of God in Him are Yes, and in Him Amen, to the glory of God through us" (2 Cor. 1:20). Notice three wonderful things Paul says in this verse. First, he speaks of all of God's promises, not just some of them. That naturally includes Old Testament promises since God's plan in Christ comes from eternity (Eph. 3:11). God's plan in Christ isn't a reaction or an example of God's "shifting gears." Therefore, the promises in the Old Testament advance that plan and are not disconnected from it. Second, all God's promises find their yes and amen in Christ, which is a way to say that all the promises receive a "Certainly!" from God due to their connection with Christ. You name the promise, it is fulfilled in Christ—His love, His advents, His person, His redemptive work, His judgment. Third, we respond to Christ's being the sole channel of God's blessings by glorifying God. When we praise God through Christ, we profess His central role in our relationship to God and also His central role in the history of redemption from the very beginning (e.g., Gen. 3:15).

When God assured Israel that it would receive rest in the Promised Land (Deut. 25:19), we should not feel excluded, as if that promise referred only to the nation of Israel. Hebrews tells us that this rest in the Promised Land was a symbol of the greater rest we have in Christ (Heb. 4:1–10). We should take comfort in the symbolism that God intended for us to see. Since all of God's promises have always been fulfilled in Christ, we should not be surprised that even earthly promises about land have their ultimate fulfillment for believers in Christ.

For another example, God promised Israel a *forever* inheritance in the Promised Land: "'I will bring back the captives of My people Israel; they shall build the waste cities and inhabit them; they shall plant vineyards and drink wine from them; they shall also make gardens and eat fruit from them. I will plant them in their land, and no longer shall they be pulled up from the land I have given them,' says the LORD your God" (Amos 9:14–15).

This promise is indeed true for Jewish believers, but other "true Jews"—that is, believers of other ethnicities—are not excluded from it. Jesus tells New Testament believers that "the meek...shall inherit the earth" (Matt. 5:5), an expansive promise that includes the Promised Land. Paul drives this expansive promise home when he says to Gentile believers, "All things are yours," including "the world" and "things present" and "things to come" (1 Cor. 3:21–23). This means that promises to Israel about something as earthly as land were never meant to be separated from God's purposes toward all His elect people in Christ. God naturally plans to give the entire world to His people since believers are joint heirs with Jesus (Rom. 8:17, 32).

All the Promises to Us and for Us

To sum up, Christians must enjoy a fundamental, overall posture to all things in the Old Testament. We should not feel excluded from it but rather feel that it is lovingly aimed directly at us, and its promises are promises to us. There will be nuance in understanding how exactly certain promises are for us, but all the promises are.

God's promises to elect Israel are emblems of His larger promises to believers in Christ from every tongue, tribe, and nation. This does not mean that every promise to Israel should be ham-fistedly applied to the church as if there were absolutely no difference between Israel and the church. And it also doesn't mean that one may ignore nuance in handling Old Testament texts. It does mean that a proper understanding of the Bible leads one to be assured that every promise found in Scripture is fulfilled in Christ in some way and therefore applies to believers in some way.

Let's look at one final example of how Old Testament texts that seem alien actually refer to Christian people. The city of Jerusalem was the capital city of Israel, also called Zion. It's clear enough that Zion refers to a location (1 Chron. 11:5). But it is also viewed as referring to the elect within that city, to people who can leave the location and go preach the good news: "O Zion, you who bring good tidings, get up into the high mountain…say to the cities of Judah, 'Behold your God!'" (Isa. 40:9). Thus, in the Old Testament, Zion can refer to both the geographic location and to the godly people who live there. With this background in mind, when the New Testament refers to Zion as the invisible church (Heb. 12:22–23), it is clear that this is not an unwarranted invention. It is grounded in the Old Testament. Even more, Zion's holy hill is used as a symbol of heaven in the Old Testament (see Ps. 2:6, 23:6). Therefore, when Zion is encouraged to rejoice (e.g., Ps. 48:11) or said to be blessed (e.g., Ps. 132:15), you are not excluded, for you are a believer, a citizen of the heavenly Zion. While Old Testament statements do have an ancient Near Eastern context, it must be remembered that Israelite institutions were intended by God to be emblems of larger realities. This idea is fundamental to having joy when you read the Old Testament. It postures you correctly as God's sheep in the green pastures of His Word. The Old Testament speaks directly to you. You are a child in God's house, not an acquaintance, a bystander, or a second-class citizen.

This presentation of biblical teaching cannot hope to answer every question that might arise about various promises in the Old Testament, but I hope it does curb a problematic and all-too-prevalent tendency of creating too great a distinction between the Testaments and of viewing the Old Testament as remote or, even worse, as alienating and dark. The Old Testament may not have as much light in it as the New Testament does, but it is no dark place, for it reveals the coming of the Light of the World who would bring salvation to the ends of the earth (e.g., Isa. 49:10). How can we not rejoice as we read it?

Study Questions

1. Have you ever felt excluded from Old Testament passages?

2. What verses teach that the Old Testament was written to New Testament believers?

3. What verses teach that the Old Testament was and is able to bring people to a saving knowledge of Christ?

4. What verses teach that Old Testament saints believed in Christ?

5. Are believers of every ethnic stock children of Abraham? How do you know?

6. What are some Old Testament passages that preach Christ and heaven?

7. Did the Old Testament preach "the gospel"? How do you know?

8. How do we know that ethnicity has nothing to do with being "God's chosen people"?

9. The chapter mentions several promises from the Old Testament that are often understood as referring only to Israel, such as the promise that Abraham's seed will be like the sand of the seashore. List some other promises that are often unduly limited this way.

10. How does this chapter make you feel about the Old Testament? How would you help someone who feels that the Old Testament is foreign and alienating?

CHAPTER 14

Joy at the Prospect of Growing Old and Dying

So also is the resurrection of the dead. The body is sown in corruption, it is raised in incorruption. It is sown in dishonor, it is raised in glory. It is sown in weakness, it is raised in power. It is sown a natural body, it is raised a spiritual body.
—1 Corinthians 15:42–44

My whole life I've heard Christians, typically elderly ones, say things like "I'm looking forward to my resurrection body"; "I sure am glad there's a new body coming to me"; "Can't wait to get my upgraded model."

There is something poignantly sad about the process of aging. When it gets advanced, many people become childlike again, and they lose their independence. What once was a strong, vital man with a light in his eyes and dreams in his heart is now a dear hunched fellow shuffling behind his walker, smiling at everyone and hardly able to remember what was said a few minutes ago. It is hard to behold it without one's heart being wrung.

You can't stave off advancing decrepitude forever. Its coming is relentless and unstoppable. If God keeps you from an early demise, weakness, frailty, and then death are what you have coming. An elderly chap might warn you to "never get old," but what choice do you have? Aside from an untimely demise or the Lord's return, it's a certainty.

There is a question before us all, especially those of us closer to the end of life: How can we rejoice at the prospect of old age and decay and death? Death is not beautiful; it is ugly and scary. It is an "enemy" (1 Cor. 15:26) and the curse for sin (Rom. 6:23). Yet we must rejoice always, even in the face of it, for the gospel reverses the curse. So how can we?

We must hold on to the promises about the resurrection, just as those elderly do. Their statements might seem like truisms, but we must not deny their truth merely because they are stated simply or sound like homespun wisdom. They sum up an assured biblical hope.

"When He is revealed, we shall be like Him, for we shall see Him as He is" (1 John 3:2). Christ "will transform our lowly body that it may be conformed to His glorious body" (Phil. 3:21). The Christian expects to be raised after the pattern of Christ's own resurrection. That truth is utterly precious. But what will the resurrection body be like? Paul answers that question in 1 Corinthians 15:35–49. We find that there will be similarity between earthly and resurrected bodies, but they will also be quite different. How will the "upgraded model" be better? What do we have to look forward to?

The Resurrection Body Will Be Far Better

The resurrection body will be *incorruptible*. "The body is sown in corruption, it is raised in incorruption" (1 Cor. 15:42). Corruption refers to decay and deterioration. The point of contrast is between the decomposition that happens in the grave and its opposite—incorruption. But deterioration begins long before the grave. The current body so easily breaks down, gets degenerative diseases, loses muscle, loses bone density, or just loses energy. It is perishable, like food that goes bad (Col. 2:21–22). But the resurrection body will not be subject to physical decline in any way. It will be imperishable.

You might wonder how a human body could ever become incorruptible. Paul appears to address that: "Foods for the stomach and the stomach for foods, but God will destroy both it and them" (1 Cor. 6:13). The Greek word for *destroy* in this verse means "to render ineffective," not "to annihilate." Paul is saying that God will render the stomach ineffective as the means for sustaining life. In heaven, just as there will be no need for a light source (Rev. 22:5), there also will be no dependence on food. Our resurrection bodies will apparently still be able to eat (Luke 24:42–43) but will not need to. Where will our energy and strength come from? God will forever connect our physical state directly to His unending supply of power. Donald Macleod writes that "the resurrection body will never be independent of God, who is Himself the source of all energy, but in its dependence it will be imperishable."[1]

In our current state we have to eat food or our bodies begin to weaken. Not so in our future state. Imagine always functioning at peak efficiency and not having to constantly feed your body in order to gain energy. Imagine not dealing with fatigue and waning strength. No decline, only health and vigor in a never-ending supply. Just as our inheritance is "incorruptible," meaning that it "does not fade away" (1 Peter 1:4), neither will our bodies degenerate from their pristine ideal condition. The glow of uncursed humanity will never fade from our resurrected, glorified bodies.

The resurrection body will be *glorious*. "It is sown in dishonor, it is raised in glory" (1 Cor. 15:43). Being "sown" or consigned to the grave is a dishonor, an indignity. But even before death, our state is inglorious too. Paul describes the body as "lowly," referring to its humiliated condition under the curse (Phil. 3:21). Our bodies are not evil, but they are certainly touched by the fall and therefore inglorious. In the resurrection this lowliness will be taken away. "It is raised in glory," Paul tells us.

One might wonder what sort of glory Paul had in mind. Does he mean brightness like the heavenly glory displayed at Christ's transfiguration, and as when angels are revealed, and as Daniel 12:3 appears to describe? Probably not. He contrasts glory with dishonor, so it is best to think of the glory he refers to as an increase of dignity. In our current condition there are all sorts of indignities, and they increase the older we get. One elderly person sat in a restaurant

---

1. Donald Macleod, *A Faith to Live By* (Geanies House, Fearn, Ross-shire: Mentor, 2002), 308–9.

waiting a long time to be served and commented, "When you get to be my age, you're invisible." That is an indignity.

In the resurrection, there will be no more indignities. Christ's redemption will fully reach the physical realm. Even the material side of man will be free from all the inglorious things that go along with our fallen condition—aging, deterioration, weakness. All the potential honor of being human will be realized. It will be glorious, not lowly and pitiable. Think of humanity reflecting God's glory in splendor, undimmed and untarnished. Human greatness will reach an apex, and we will be what we should be, and it will be all of God.

The resurrection body will be *powerful*. "It is sown in weakness, it is raised in power" (1 Cor. 15:43). The word translated *weakness* refers to incapacity or inability to function. It undoubtedly refers to the inactivity of the corpse as it is buried or "sown" in the ground. In the Gospels, "weakness" refers to physical illness too, and it is a glorious truth that the resurrection body will not suffer ailments anymore: "There shall be no more death, nor sorrow, nor crying. There shall be no more pain" (Rev. 21:4). In 2 Corinthians 12:10 the term *weak* refers to the state of being vulnerable to external harm, including insults and deprivation.

The human body now is internally (physically) weak and also externally weak, or vulnerable to harm from outside sources. But it will be raised in power, capacity, and ability. This certainly refers to physical strength, but Christ will rule the nations with a rod of iron, so His people will be empowered from without too; there will be no more weakness due to external vulnerability. Isolation and lack of help will be gone, and Christ's people will no longer be as sheep among wolves. Everything about the future state will be powerful.

The resurrection body will be *spiritual*. "It is sown a natural body, it is raised a spiritual body" (1 Cor. 15:44). The contrast between natural and spiritual is not to be misunderstood as between the spiritual and the physical. To say it is sown as physical and raised as spiritual might be interpreted to mean that the resurrection body is noncorporeal, like a ghost. That is not what Paul means. The New Testament often contrasts spiritual with carnal, or sinful.

For example, Paul said to the Corinthians, "I…could not speak to you as to spiritual people but as to carnal, as to babes in Christ…. For where there are envy, strife, and divisions among you, are you not carnal?" (1 Cor. 3:1, 3). In 1 Corinthians 15:44 the contrast is not between spiritual and carnal but rather between spiritual and natural, but *natural* often carries a similar moral association as *carnal* (see 1 Cor. 2:14; James 3:15; Jude 19). The body as it is now is natural—that is, connected to the Adamic, fallen nature.

The body is not evil, but it is a tool of evil, because people are born influenced by the world, the flesh, and the devil (Eph. 2:1–3). Christians, though, have already been translated from the kingdom of darkness into the kingdom of God's dear Son (Col. 1:13). But we have not yet experienced the final step in our deliverance from all evil—the resurrection of our bodies. When we are resurrected, the body will be free from evil influences and will become a perfectly fit tool for the Holy Spirit. It will be spiritual and no longer natural. At present, it is hampered in serving Christ because of evil influences but also because of simple weakness. Desire to pray or read the Word is sabotaged by weariness and distraction. Illness spoils a chance to share the gospel. Weakness keeps you from helping someone. Bad hearing keeps you from understanding what people say. Singing with too much gusto makes you light-headed! But the resurrection body will be a fit tool for the Spirit of God. Think of yourself and your influences always encouraging you in the right course rather than opposing you. All that is weak, natural, and carnal will be gone, and the body will no longer clog the free exercise of love for God and man.

How to Reflect on Heaven

Recently I was sitting with an elderly person who was talking about looking forward to heaven. We both agreed that heaven was going to be really great, but he was having a hard time thinking beyond the general idea that heaven will be way better than life is now. My heart went out to him as he fought his dementia, and I wanted to help him gain more encouragement from thoughts of heaven. I considered for a moment, and it came to me: "A good way to think of heaven is to think of all the negatives in this life, the things that make it miserable, and to remember that heaven will be the opposite of those things. Any painful thing can become a reflection on glory to come." His eyes brightened, and he jabbed an excited finger at me as he said, "Yeah!" We then proceeded to reflect together, in essence canceling out miserable things with thoughts of heaven: no more illness, weakness, pain, unmet needs, sorrow, loss, uncertainty about the future, long-delayed gratification, confusion, temptation, or sin. It brought joy to think in a very simple way how God will fully reverse the curse when He resurrects believers. What life will be like then!

Many people wallow in grief when they lose a loved one. Grief can be potent indeed. Jesus Himself wept at the death of Lazarus when He saw its effect on his sisters, Mary and Martha. Yet we might abuse the Lord's compassion for mourners to justify faithless sorrow. Christians must not grieve as if there were no salvation or heaven. Paul told Christians not to "sorrow as others who have no hope" (1 Thess. 4:13). The fall and its curse must not overwhelm the joy of Christ's redemption. We also must not be embittered at the death of a loved one we fear is unsaved. As crushing as such a loss is, a person's eternal fate is above our pay grade, and we must not meddle with matters too great for us (Ps. 131:1). We must love them and pray for them and evangelize them when they are alive, then leave them in God's hands once they pass on.

God made humankind with bodies, and therefore our ideal state is physical. Though the fall has had severe effects on the body, even to the point where many have desired to be free from it forever, God has determined to advance Christ's redemption so far that even our bodies will be recovered. God will complete His salvation when He brings about the "redemption of our body" (Rom. 8:23). The eternal state is a bodily existence, and it is crucial we hold on to that if we want to properly conceive of heaven.

As we grow old, we feel that we are entering a frightening dark place, for we experience deterioration, indignity, and weakness.

But we must embrace joy at the promise of Christ's final and total redemption. We already have redemption, but there is a final stage of it that is not yet consummated, and we eagerly wait for it. In the meantime, we have the blessing of abiding with and faithfully serving the One who comes to make our bodies like His. Though we grow old and weak, our Savior does not change, and He will never leave us.

Study Questions

1. Is death natural and beautiful, or is it a curse to be mourned?

2. This chapter is about rejoicing at the prospect of death. How can it be that Christians can rejoice at a curse to be mourned?

3. What does it mean that the resurrection body will be incorruptible?

4. What does it mean that the resurrection body will be glorious?

5. What does it mean that the resurrection body will be powerful?

6. What does it mean that the resurrection body will be spiritual?

7. What are some negatives in this life that will be negated by the resurrection?

8. How would you help someone who thinks of mankind's permanent heavenly condition as nonphysical or ghostly?

CHAPTER 15

Biblical Joy
versus Cheap Joy

*This is he who hears the word and immediately receives it with
joy; yet he has no root in himself, but endures only for a while.
For when tribulation or persecution arises because of the word,
immediately he stumbles.*
                                        —Matthew 13:20–21

These verses from Matthew tell us that a person can receive the Word
of God with joy and still ultimately fall away and prove to be an unbeliever. The unbelieving Herod is said to have listened happily to the
preaching of John the Baptist—"he…heard him gladly" (Mark 6:20;
cf. John 5:35)—before he ordered him to be decapitated. Joy, even
in spiritual things, is not an infallible evidence of true Christianity.

Two Sorts of Joy

After all this teaching on joy, do we now see it isn't necessary? By no
means! Joy in Christ is crucial. It's one of the segments of the Spirit's
fruit. Paul would not say "rejoice in the Lord always" if it weren't vital.

But it is also true that the presence of joy, or gladness, is not
a guarantee of the Spirit's presence. Joy (that is, of a certain sort)
should always be present in believers, but gladness can be and is
present in unbelievers. It is dangerous to evaluate yourself and think,
"I am happy about spiritual things, therefore I know I am spiritually
healthy." The Puritan John Flavel made this point very effectively:

> There is nothing more apt to produce soul-destroying con-
> fidence than the stirrings of our affections about spiritual
> things, while the heart remains unrenewed. Such a person

seems to have all that is required of a Christian, and to have attained the purpose of knowledge—its influence upon the heart and affections. Indeed, such a poor deluded soul thinks, "If I heard, read, or prayed...with a dead, cold, and unconcerned heart; or if I made a show of zeal and affection...well might I suspect myself to be a hypocrite. But it is not so with me. I feel my heart melted many times when I read the sufferings of Christ. I find my heart raised and ravished with strange joys and comforts when I hear the glory of heaven in the gospel.... I have often heard ministers cautioning and warning their people not to rest satisfied with idle and speculative notions in their understandings, but to labor for impressions upon their hearts. This I have attained.... Therefore I am in a most safe condition."[1]

If a person can have such joy even in spiritual things and still be a spiritual castaway, how can I know my joy isn't false joy? How can I "rejoice in the Lord always" and be assured that my joy is genuine fruit of the Holy Spirit and evidence of His power and presence? Consider the following four points in answer to these very important questions.

How to Know if Your Joy Is Biblical

Accept that joy can be neutral, worthless, or even evil. This is a basic starting point. Joy can be stirred up by any happy story. I've heard people say that this shouldn't even be called joy but rather happiness or perhaps fun. I'm not so concerned with the term but with the idea that some joy is in fact cheap. People find great joy in a sport or hobby and are always seeking their happy place—their boat, their favorite fishing hole, their favorite game. The philosopher Friedrich Nietzsche famously said that the "last men" would be people who laughed in the face of humanity's despair without a desire to better themselves.[2] Happiness, cheer, and laughter are no guaranteed

---

1. Lightly adapted from John Flavel, *Fountain of Life*, 305–6.
2. Friedrich Nietzsche, *Thus Spoke Zarathustra*, trans. R. J. Hollingdale (London: Penguin, 1988), 46–47.

blessings. In fact, they can be a ripened fruit of the curse, ones that are especially damning. When the Israelites at the time of Isaiah chose to eat, drink, and be merry even though God's judgment was looming, they chose joy instead of repentance. God responded by judging them without mercy (Isa. 22:13–14).

Be sure your joy flows from deep conviction of sin and repentance. "Lament and mourn and weep," James tells believers who are caught and ensnared in sin (James 4:9). People who have not trusted Christ and sorrowed over their sin are incapable of joy that pleases God. Without faith we can do nothing that pleases Him (Heb. 11:6), least of all rejoice. Rejoicing without repenting is like laughing at the gates of hell. The wrath of God is coming, and all people will stand before God, but the unbeliever ignores that and giggles. No wonder Solomon said that attempting to enjoy mirth without being right with God is "madness" (Eccl. 2:2). Nothing can be right with a person until that person deals with the great fact of eternal judgment.

There is a profound seriousness to life in this world. Life is ticking away, and people are storing up wrath for the day of judgment even as they pretend such a day will never come. Biblical joy arises only from a good look at the gravity of a fallen world and our own tragic contribution to it. It arises by believing that God can bring good out of things, even for me, and He has done so through the cross. Any other joy is flippant, short-lived, and doomed to turn to wailing and gnashing of teeth. Joy that doesn't flow from conviction of sin and repentance is insupportable.

The truth that biblical joy must flow from conviction and repentance is very meaningful for Christian thought and life. First, it is obvious that you must repent and be converted before you can properly rejoice. Furthermore, if sin has crept back into your life after conversion, you must repent again in order for your joy to be pleasing to God. If you tolerate evil, your joy becomes emotional antinomianism, a sort of celebrating while flouting God's law and making light of sin. Finally, joy in this life should be accompanied by watchfulness; there is no carefree unguardedness in this life for a believer who takes seriously his fight against sin and need to mortify

the flesh. Life is a battleground, not a playground. We must rejoice—
and thank God we have reason to do so constantly, for Christ has
gained the victory—but we must do so watchfully, for our enemy
seeks to devour us, and our flesh is always ready to open the gate of
the soul to him.

See if your joy exists alongside power over sin. We are no longer
speaking of repentance from sin but rather continued empowerment against it. Believers will admittedly never be completely free of
evil in this life, and sin beleaguers the thoughts, words, actions, and
feelings of the godliest saints. But it is also true that Christians are
guaranteed massive empowerment over sin (Rom. 6:14; Gal. 5:16;
1 John 5:4). Believers must never lose sight of this, or else a life-
destroying antinomianism will result in which a person can go on
his way "taking joy" in Christ yet fraternizing with His enemy. Such
a prospect ought to evoke abhorrence in the hearts of those who love
the Lord. "You who love the LORD, hate evil!" (Ps. 97:10). Biblical joy
coexists with an adamant rejection of sin and substantial empowerment over it.

Despite the lurking danger of cheap grace, the point here
is worthy of instant rejoicing—the gospel does indeed promise
empowerment over sin. There is no victory without struggle, but
there is victory indeed. It is crucial to simply and joyfully believe and
accept the promise of empowerment and then, with faith fixed joyfully on the promise, go forth and fight the Lord's battle against sin.
"Be strong in the Lord and in the power of His might" (Eph. 6:10).
There is no other way to do battle, for only faith wins the victory. To
fail to joyfully receive this promise of empowerment is to lose the
battle before even beginning to fight.

*Examine yourself and see if your joy finds its greatest happiness
in seeking Christ in heaven.* "Set your mind on things above, not on
things on the earth" (Col. 3:2). True joy is rooted in salvation, focuses
on Christ, lingers on thoughts of His presence in heaven, and looks
forward to His return. These things are simply statements of biblical
doctrine. Therefore, nothing is more important for us than to know
biblical doctrine and respond to it experientially with joy. Paul loved

the Philippians as his own soul, yet he said it was far preferable to him to die and go be with Christ (Phil. 1:23). His attitude reflects a heart that was hidden in heaven with Christ, his treasure.

Joy Must Not Be an Idol

Christ died so that we would value Him more than anyone or anything. Loving Him most means earnestly pursuing Him, making His Word our law, and prioritizing our relationship with Him over relationship with others: "He who loves father or mother more than Me is not worthy of Me. And he who loves son or daughter more than Me is not worthy of Me" (Matt. 10:37). These words in Matthew are crucial because Jesus was prioritizing relationship with Him, even over those whom we value most in the world.

True biblical joy is found in a context of loving Him most. If we come to love something else more than Him, our joy has become cheap. We must eagerly, earnestly seek Christ and be attached to Him, longing for His presence and anticipating being with Him in glory. Cheap joy fiddles about with delighting in things of earth while having very little warmth or attraction to the biblical Jesus. Nothing is more important than to grow in love to Christ (1 Cor. 16:22).

Is your joy biblical or is it cheap? Here are some absolute tests: (1) Do you recognize that some joy is simply wrong? (2) Does your joy coexist with conviction of sin? (3) Does your joy coexist with power over sin, not perfectly but substantially? (4) Is Christ in heaven the subject in which you rejoice?

The bottom line is simple: when people just want to be happy, their joy doesn't please God, who is holy, takes sin seriously, and is offended at humanity's idolatry. True joy always coincides with repentance and growth in holiness, without which no one will see the Lord (Heb. 12:14). And true joy is joy in Christ. Frances Brook put it very poignantly and memorably in her hymn "My Goal Is God Himself": "My goal is God Himself, not joy, nor peace, not even blessing but Himself, my God."

Study Questions

1. Matthew 13:20–21 provides the teaching on which this chapter is based. What is its main idea? How does Mark 6:20 contribute?

2. How do Friedrich Nietzsche and the prophet Isaiah show us that happiness can be sinful?

3. Why is it important for you to recognize that cheap, ungodly joy is a real thing?

4. Why can't you have biblical joy until you have come under conviction and repented?

5. Why must biblical joy exist alongside power over sin?

6. Why must biblical joy be focused on Christ and heaven?

7. Consider the statement, "My goal is God Himself, not joy, nor peace, not even blessing but Himself, my God." Does this reflect your heart? Or do you seek God in order to gain something else, essentially making Him a tool for getting something that is greater to you than He is? Do you need to repent of idolatry and recommit to putting God first?

CHAPTER 16

Joy Even When
Society Disintegrates

God is our refuge and strength, a very present help in trouble.
Therefore we will not fear, even though the earth be removed,
and though the mountains be carried into the midst of the sea.

—Psalm 46:1–2

It goes without saying that societal disintegration tempts believers to lose their joy. At the time of this writing, it is toward the end of 2020. America has experienced a pandemic, quarantines, massive job losses, rioting, looting, widespread street violence, and large-scale distrust in our political processes. And it doesn't look like things are going to get better anytime soon, though one can always hope. There seem to be a lot of dark events in the world right now.

It is easy to get depressed or feel dread. What does the future hold? Will I be able to support my family? What will the world be like for my kids? How much more pressure can this nation bear before splitting apart at the seams? These and other questions raise the specter of uncertainty about our safety and prosperity, and we begin to fear that Misery is confronting us like an assailant we cannot fight.

Are you struggling with your current cultural climate and agonizing over it? You might be tempted to respond in a multitude of ways: getting into fiery Twitter wars, heading for the hills with your bugout bag, swallowing conspiracy theories, losing yourself in entertainment, shrilly venting to all your friends. The human heart can respond in many ways to dark things in the world.

In trying times we need a word from God to give us reasons to remain joyful in all situations, "giving thanks always for all things to God the Father" (Eph. 5:20). Many, many Scripture passages give us solid reasons. In fact, a fruitful approach to Bible study in general is to read it with that question mind: What rationale does this passage give for being joyful in dark places? A key passage that deals specifically with the issue of joy when society disintegrates is Psalm 46.

Stability in God during Societal Disintegration

The setting of Psalm 46 is cultural upheaval and societal disintegration—wars and the fall of nations. The psalm describes these things using metaphors of natural disasters, like mountains being "carried into the midst of the sea" and quaking at the seas' roaring (v. 2). The psalmist imagines apocalyptic events, not because he expects them to happen anytime soon but because they are apt emblems for the thing he has in his mind, societal upheaval. You can see that this is the setting of the psalm because it moves past metaphor: "the nations raged, the kingdoms were moved" (v. 6). This is upheaval (nations raging) and disintegration (kingdoms being moved). In such tumultuous times, people feel their vulnerability, and fear infests society at every level. People need a Rock.

The psalm's main theme is the stability that comes from being in covenant with God. Three times it anchors the soul on God's covenant: "God is our refuge and strength.... The LORD of hosts is with us.... The God of Jacob is our refuge" (vv. 1, 7, 11). The most basic biblical expression of the covenant is the statement that God is our God, and we are His people. The Bible often varies this by using illustrative imagery for God: "my fortress," "my rock," "my shield." Notice the relational meaning these possessive pronouns carry. It might be helpful to use an example from common experience: saying "a wife" is very different from saying "my wife." That one pronoun changes everything. It expresses the unique relationship of a covenant. Saying "God is our refuge" and "God is our strength" refers to God's role in His covenant with us. Once you've seen the psalm's overall covenantal emphasis, the question becomes what specific blessings we can expect from being in covenant with God. Let's take a look at three blessed things the psalm gives us.

Three Blessings of the Covenant

The first covenant blessing is that God is "a very present help in trouble" (v. 1). If you said someone was "very present," you'd undoubtedly mean something like "he's always there." One translation offered "abundantly available" as a possible rendering. In other words, God is the opposite of distant, remote, or detached. But the psalm isn't merely saying that God is present. What good is having someone close by if they don't help? It would provide moral support but little else. The psalm specifies that it is God's help that is not remote. He provides abundantly available help to His people. The experiential result of accepting this fact is that "we will not fear" (v. 2), even in the face of earth-shattering disasters and disorder.

Do you feel like God's help is ever-present, or do you feel like He hardly ever helps you? It is vital for your spiritual health not just to believe that God's help is ever present but to find your refuge in that fact. If you do not, when earth-shattering events occur, you will rely on yourself, your strength, your wisdom, or that of other people. "Cursed is the man who trusts in man.... 'Blessed is the man who trusts in the LORD'" (Jer. 17:5, 7). If you view yourself as cut off from God's help, you will not trust Him, for you feel He isn't there for you. Why trust a god who doesn't help? Refresh your faith in God as He has revealed Himself to be. Even in the worst trials your fearful imagination can conjure up, God is your refuge and strength.

The second covenant blessing is that God dedicates His omnipotence to bless His people (Ps. 46:4–7). This marvelous thought is explained regarding its experiential results (v. 4) and timing (v. 5), and then it is stated outright (v. 6).

The experiential results of God's help are compared to a river. "There is a river whose streams shall make glad the city of God." If you've ever wondered about this river imagery, just contrast it with the raging tumult in verse 3. There is disorder and disaster in the world on a cataclysmic scale. But for people who are in covenant

with God, those in "the city of God," life is like resting by a tran-
quil river. It's a stark contrast—mountains thrown into raging seas,
followed by a river of serenity. This expression shows the joy that
results from being in covenant with God. The ultimate experience of
this will be in heaven, but we are to experience massive joy now (Gal.
5:22). Peace like a river is already and not yet.

The timing of God's help corrects our impatient culture. I
imagine that some Christian people want to accept that God is an
ever-present help, but they hesitate because, deep down, they feel
like God rarely helps them. If you feel like this, the psalm speaks in a
special way to you: "God shall help her, just at the break of dawn" (Ps.
46:5). This speaks to those who feel like God lets them struggle in a
trial that never ends—an interminable, everlasting dark place. But a
dawn is coming, and trials have an end. Troubles are not everlasting,
no matter how we may feel. God allows the trial to last as long as He
thinks best and then brings in help at the right time for those who
wait for Him, "just at the break of dawn." We must not be demanding as to God's timing or indignant when His help tarries; rather, we
humbly and hopefully wait for God's dawn to break and shed light on
the dark places. God is all-wise, and help will come in His good time.

The help that God brings is stated outright as the help of omnipotence. "The nations raged…He uttered His voice, the earth melted"
(v. 6). This shows the greatness of the help; God "has made over" His
almighty power to bless believers.[1] The earth melting depicts God's
powerful salvation. The earth was heaving at the nations' rage but
will melt at the mere sound of God's voice "as snow before the sun,
or fat cast into the fire."[2] Can you imagine yourself sitting around a
campfire and tossing a bit of bacon fat onto a blazing log? It would
almost instantly melt and disappear. That is the nations; they have
no strength or substance before God's power. How important, therefore, to give weight to God and not to the day's agitating crowds!

---

1. See Strong, *Discourse of the Two Covenants*, 265.
2. David Dickson, *Psalms* (1653–55; repr., Edinburgh: Banner of Truth, 1995),
1:268.

People think great things of themselves, but they really are just scuttling about on this globe for a short time before dying and standing before God. People are not to be feared. There is something delightful in contemplating God's great power. Nothing thrills a child more than seeing his father's power as long as the child is assured of his father's love.

To sum up the second covenant blessing, God dedicates His omnipotence to helping His people; this truth should bring us peace like a river as we trust that His help will come at just the right time. The raging and agitating nations are powerless before our great God, and we should not fear them.

The third covenant blessing is that God's sovereign providence is purposeful (Ps. 46:8–11). The psalmist views the desolations in the earth from a God-centered perspective. God "made desolations in the earth" (v. 8) and brings wars to an end (v. 9). Most importantly, His providential control is purposeful. Events are not random; dark times are not arbitrary. God is guiding history forward and doing so according to plan. "Be still, and know that I am God" must be interpreted in light of the rest of the verse: "I will be exalted among the nations, I will be exalted in the earth!" (v. 10).

The statement is meant for the nations and for the godly. The nations are to stop raging and come to know God, and God's people are to stop fretting, for He controls events and is ordering them to accomplish His purpose of glorifying Himself. Believers should not join the raging nations. Though tumult is in the earth, love, joy, and peace should be in Christians' hearts. God will be glorified.

It might seem strange to gain comfort by remembering that God will glorify Himself. You might expect comfort to sound more like "Be still, for I will protect you," not "Be still, for I will be glorified." But if people are made to glorify God, then a Christian, who is a new creation with godly desires, will want God's glory more than anything. In other words, these words of the Lord here in Psalm 46 are most comforting. Nothing brings more peace and joy in the dark places than knowing that darkness cannot reach God's throne, and God is bending His omnipotence to ensure His will is done.

Even when cataclysmic things happen and society threatens to disintegrate, nothing is out of God's control. God is exercising His providence to accomplish His purposes. "The earth will be filled with the knowledge of the glory of the LORD, as the waters cover the sea" (Hab. 2:14).

Covenant Blessings in Christ

The blessings of Psalm 46 are guaranteed to us in Jesus Christ. This psalm shares imagery with Psalm 2. In both you see God responding similarly to a tumultuous world. The nations are raging (2:1; 46:6). God gives the ends of the earth to Christ, who breaks them in pieces (2:8–9). He speaks to the earth and it melts (46:6). The nations are offered peace if they will trust Christ (2:12). They are told to be still and recognize God (46:10). These parallels highlight that the judgment and gospel communicated in Psalm 46 ought to be understood in light of Psalm 2. Though Christ is not mentioned in Psalm 46, He is definitely there. How will God be exalted in the nations except by Jesus Christ as He brings redemption for His people and judgment on the wicked?

We may be in dark places, and we may not know how much longer it will be before dawn breaks, but in the meantime we can raise a joyful song and rest assured. Christ is our refuge, and He will bring light on the dark places of the earth. He will bring God's omnipotence to the help of His people. And He will return so that every knee will bow to the Father's glory. We can have great joy, even when society disintegrates, as long as we keep our gaze on Him.

Study Questions

1. How are you tempted to respond to your current cultural climate?

2. Read a psalm, a passage from the Gospels, or an epistle and then answer the question, "What rationale does this passage give for being joyful in dark places?"

3. What is the setting and main theme of Psalm 46?

4. How do we inevitably respond when we feel that God doesn't help us very much? List ways that Psalm 46 asserts that God's help is near.

5. What is the point of Psalm 46's river imagery?

6. The earth melting is imagery designed to depict God's powerful salvation. How should we respond to the truth of God's almighty power over the earth and the nations?

7. "Be still, and know that I am God" should be interpreted by the next statement: "I will be exalted." Why is His determination to exalt Himself a reason to be still? And how should the nations and the godly respond differently by being still?

8. How do we know that the blessings mentioned in Psalm 46 are fulfilled in Christ?

CHAPTER 17

Joy at the Last Judgment

For the Son of Man will come in the glory of His Father with His angels, and then He will reward each according to his works.
—Matthew 16:27

To be prepared for the last judgment, it helps to know what to expect, especially what Christ's standard of judgment will be. Scripture answers consistently by telling us that Christ will judge all people according to what they have done—that is, according to their works. From the Old Testament to the New, this is how the Bible consistently speaks, and it does so of believers and unbelievers alike:

To You, O Lord, belongs mercy; for You render to each one according to his work. (Ps. 62:12)

[God] "will render to each one according to his deeds." (Rom. 2:6)

We must all appear before the judgment seat of Christ, that each one may receive the things done in the body, according to what he has done, whether good or bad. (2 Cor. 5:10)

Behold, I am coming quickly, and My reward is with Me, to give to every one according to his work. (Rev. 22:12)

If you believe that God will give you a pass at judgment because you are a Christian, you are clearly mistaken. He will not say, "You are a believer, so you won't be judged." On the contrary, He will judge you according to your works.

But this raises an obvious question: How does this judgment square with forgiveness of sin and salvation by faith? After being justified by faith without the deeds of the law (Rom. 3:28), are we facing a strict accounting for our works after all? Is our eternal fate riding on our performance?

Believers will face a judgment according to their works but not a judgment that determines whether their fate will be life or death. Theirs will not be a judgment in which condemnation remains a possibility. Believers must not imagine a courtroom in which the words might thunder forth, "guilty as charged." Instead of this dreadful scenario, believers will have their fruit evaluated so as to receive the proper reward. The judgment they receive is an assessment. This is crucial because Christians might think of judgment as having a nail-biting uncertainty to it. They might think they'll end up damned after all. This invites dread into one's life and denies the gospel's assurances.

Will the Judgment Be Different for Believers?

Is there evidence in the Bible that Christians' judgment will be fundamentally different from that of unbelievers? Without a definitive answer to this question, the thought of the last judgment will inhibit your joy. Thankfully, there is definitive evidence. Consider four Scriptures that are representative of many others.

Christians presently enjoy justification and peace with God: "Having been justified by faith, we have peace with God through our Lord Jesus Christ" (Rom. 5:1). Justification (being declared righteous before God) and its resultant peace are enjoyed now. Believers do not have to wait for a future end-times justification.

This presently enjoyed salvation means that believers cannot be condemned: "There is therefore now no condemnation to those who are in Christ Jesus" (Rom. 8:1). The word *now* means "at the present time," so Paul is describing Christians as currently "uncondemnable."

Furthermore, eternal life cannot be lost once it is gained: "My sheep hear My voice...I give them eternal life, and they shall never perish" (John 10:27–28). Charles Spurgeon once said that it is impossible to understand the words "my sheep will never perish" in any other way than to believe that saved people cannot be lost, ever.

Finally, believers will not come to judgment: "Most assuredly, I say to you, he who hears My word and believes in Him who sent Me has everlasting life, and shall not come into judgment, but has passed from death into life" (John 5:24). The fate of Christians is not uncertain.

Of course, the fate of unbelievers is not up in the air either. Their judgment will not be an investigation into whether they should be considered worthy of heaven. God says they are "condemned already" (John 3:18). For them, judgment will involve the inescapable enforcement of God's righteous death sentence. They will be judged according to their works in the strictness of the covenant of works, in which one failure brings death (Gal. 3:10). For them judgment will bring condemnation—the "sentence of God, condemning a man to bear the punishment of…eternal wrath for sin."[1] This is exactly what Jesus assured unbelievers: "He who does not believe is condemned" (John 3:18).

Believers, however, cannot be condemned, are gloriously secure for eternity, and therefore will not encounter a stern judge. They will be gathered into the arms of their heavenly Father. For them judgment will involve a generous evaluation of their works, for their sins have been washed away, and since they have been brought into God's family, He will treat them as loved ones. Jesus gives a glimpse of this generosity when He says that even a cup of cold water given in His name will receive a just reward (Mark 9:41). God will reward the smallest acts of service. Believers' sins will of course be taken into account (1 Cor. 3:10–15). But those sins will have already been forgiven, and so the difference between the judgment of believers and unbelievers couldn't be more stark. Both are technically a judgment according to works, but what a relief for believers!

Have you missed out on experiencing the joy God wants you to have because you secretly dread judgment? Let the full implications

---

1. Flavel, *Method of Grace*, 511.

of the gospel flood your soul with peace, and rejoice at your heavenly Father's love for you. Believers in Christ really are saved from the wrath to come: "Having now been justified by His blood, we shall be saved from wrath through Him" (Rom. 5:9).

Someone might wonder if there are any surprises waiting for believers after death. Paul says that Christians will be judged according to what we've done, "whether good or bad" (2 Cor. 5:10). Will judgment involve some sort of limited punishment for bad things we've done? The Bible teaches that, for believers, the afterlife will include nothing but joy. First Corinthians 3:13–15 speaks of their judgment in terms of a "fire," but it refers to burning Christians' unworthy deeds, not the Christians themselves. There is no purgatory. Jesus assured the thief on the cross that, after placing his faith in Christ, he would be with Him in "Paradise" that very day (Luke 23:43). Paul assured believers that "to be absent from the body" is "to be present with the Lord" (2 Cor. 5:8). The statement "whether good or bad" can simply mean that believers who bore more fruit in life will gain greater reward in heaven. Christ took the punishment for all our sin on the cross (Col. 2:13–14); therefore, no punishment is left for believers. As John Flavel wrote, "If you are freed from condemnation, you shall stand with boldness at the judgment-seat of Christ."[2]

First Corinthians 4 also mentions the judgment in terms that seem, on the face of it, disturbing. When the Lord comes He will "bring to light the hidden things of darkness and reveal the counsels of the hearts" (v. 5). This language can easily conjure up dreadful images: an investigation, a shocking exposé for all to see, divine disgust, and the damnation of the soul. Joy cannot coexist with these thoughts. But Paul immediately points away from such grim pictures. Christ's bringing to light hidden things will have a certain result: "Then each one's praise will come from God" (v. 5). Paul couches language about the judgment of believers in hopeful terms, and so should we. The evaluation of believers' secrets will result in

---

2. Flavel, *Method of Grace*, 518.

reward. A Christian must never lose sight of that, or else joy dies in the soul as the gospel is not enjoyed in its true power.

An important caveat should not cancel out the assurances we've been discussing. Some people at the judgment will discover that theirs will be the judgment of an unbeliever, not a believer.

Not everyone who says to Me, "Lord, Lord," shall enter the kingdom of heaven, but he who does the will of My Father in heaven. Many will say to Me in that day, "Lord, Lord, have we not prophesied in Your name, cast out demons in Your name, and done many wonders in Your name?" And then I will declare to them, "I never knew you; depart from Me, you who practice lawlessness!" (Matt. 7:21–23)

Instead of allowing such Scripture texts to unsettle you about your fate, renounce sin and reaffirm your faith in Christ and His redemptive work, which perfects you forever (Heb. 10:14). Any time sin and judgment cast a shadow, the answer is always the gospel's light. Unbelief can be defined as failing to accept the gospel as it is revealed. Therefore, embrace God's glorious promises once more. Rest again in the joy of what Christ is for your soul. But further, hear the words of the apostle Paul: "Examine yourselves as to whether you are in the faith. Test yourselves" (2 Cor. 13:5). People who believe the gospel receive the Spirit, who never fails to make progress in sanctifying the lives of believers (Rom. 6:14). Repent once more of the sin that still clings to you, rely on Christ, commit to pursuing growth, and rejoice in the progress you've made by the Spirit.

Believers' judgment will be a joyous affair of generous assessment and gracious reward in which their sins, though taken into account, will be seen as forgiven in Christ. The prospect of the last judgment is not incompatible with joy and should actually be anticipated with delight, not dread. We should love the very thought of His appearing (2 Tim. 4:8). Do you?

Anticipate Judgment with Joy

Christians can fail to rejoice in Christ because they focus more on what they do for Him than what He did (and still does and will do) for them. They have an undue emphasis on their own works. Christ's person and work provide "every spiritual blessing," and thus He meets every one of our spiritual needs (Eph. 1:3). Christ and His work are sufficient. Believers "are complete in Him" (Col. 2:10); that is, they do not need anything more than Christ and what He provides by uniting us with Himself. People fear the last judgment because they either do not see how Christ is enough or they can't bring themselves to really rest in that fact. They want joy and peace, but Jesus alone provides a basis for these things. We cannot have them if we are not fixing our eyes on Him. We must get busy filling our hearts and minds with Christ by faith. Our attentions, like anchors, will attach to something. Best have our anchor grip the Rock.

To find rest in Jesus, Christians must seek out what the Bible says about His perfect work and what it does for believers. Here are four aspects of His work that we will explore: He obeyed the law to provide righteousness for me, suffered the curse for me, ever lives to intercede for me, and will uphold His advocacy for me at the judgment. Christians must exercise faith in these things, see them with their spiritual eye, and feed their souls on them. "May the God of hope fill you with all joy and peace in believing" as we consider these four truths (Rom. 15:13).

Christ Obeyed to Provide Righteousness for Me

Christ was born subject to His own law for the purpose of saving those condemned by it. He was "born under the law, to redeem those who were under the law" (Gal. 4:4–5). Christ was born under the moral law; that is, He was obligated to obey it. But He did not enter into this obligation for Himself; He did it to benefit His people, to redeem us from the law's condemnation. Hebrews 10:7 tells us that Jesus exclaimed, "Behold, I have come…to do Your will, O God" when He came into the world. What will did He come to obey? The context says He came to obey the law (Heb. 10:8–9).

A lot of people wonder whether Christ's obedience mentioned in these texts refers to His righteous life or just to His death on the cross. The Hebrews passage we referred to above clearly focuses on

His death (Heb. 10:7–9). Every orthodox Christian believes that His perfect obedience made His sacrifice on the cross effective: His righteous life made Him a lamb "without spot" (1 Peter 1:19). But did Christ also obey to provide believers a righteousness to make up for their lack of it? A good way to grasp this question is to ask yourself, "When I think about my salvation, do I take comfort in Christ's righteous life imputed to my account?"

This distinction is commonly known as the difference between Christ's passive obedience (His death on the cross that paid the penalty due to me for my sin) and His active obedience (His righteous life imputed to my account that makes up for my lack of merit). One says that Christ died to deal with the curse against me. The other says that Christ obeyed to provide me active merit.

At the close of his all-too-short life, J. Gresham Machen, the well-known Presbyterian theologian, took great comfort in Christ's active obedience. His last words were almost in shorthand, dictated in a telegram to a friend: "I'm so thankful for active obedience of Christ. No hope without it."[3] Many godly Christians have accepted and relished not just Christ's death, as precious as that is, but His life too. When the American Puritan John Cotton wrote his catechism, "Spiritual Milk for American Babes," he asked, "How does Christ Redeem and save you?" His answer is fuller than many in our day might put it. Cotton said Christ saves "by his righteous life, bitter death, and glorious resurrection." Such an answer goes far in showing how Christ's various actions and phases of life contribute to our salvation. But the question remains: Does the Bible teach this fuller view? Does Scripture teach the active obedience of Christ?

Christ's active obedience doesn't appear in the Bible as often as His passive obedience, but it is taught. The following seven points make a cumulative case that demonstrates its reality.

---

3. Ned Stonehouse, *J. Gresham Machen: A Biographical Memoir* (1954; repr., Willow Grove, Pa.: Committee for the Historian of the Orthodox Presbyterian Church, 2017), 451.

First, Christ lived a sinless life. He was "without sin" (Heb. 4:15; 1 Peter 2:22). This is a basic starting point and leads naturally to the next point.

Second, Christ perfectly conformed to the law. "Sin is lawlessness" (1 John 3:4). The law defines righteousness as well as sin. Therefore, to say He was sinless is to say He conformed to the law. Christ conformed to it at His birth (Luke 2:21–22, 27), His baptism (Matt. 3:15), His entire ministry (John 17:4), and at His death (John 19:30). Paul speaks of His obedience as lifelong and culminating at the cross, where He "became obedient to the point of death" (Phil. 2:8). Christ obeyed all the way to the point of allowing Himself to be crucified. Together, these passages show us that Christ's obedience referred to His whole life, not just His death, though the cross was the climactic example of it.

Third, Christ obeyed the law as a substitute. His circumcision mentioned in Luke 2 and baptism, mentioned in Matthew 3, symbolized salvation (Col. 2:11–12), which Christ didn't need. Therefore, we're already seeing a substitutionary element in play. He was born under the law in order to keep it and redeem those under its condemnation. Of course, it could still be that all of His lifelong obedience functioned only to prepare Christ to be the spotless lamb. But the next few points demonstrate that there is more to it.

Fourth, believers receive a righteousness from God: "Not having my own righteousness, which is from the law, but that which is through faith in Christ, the righteousness which is from God by faith" (Phil. 3:9). Paul says his righteousness is not derived from doing works but by faith in Christ. Among other things, he's telling us that salvation is about gaining righteousness. Yes, thank God, Christ suffered the penalty for my sins on the cross, taking my curse there, but it is also true that when I believe in Christ, I gain righteousness. Have you, like Machen, included this thought in your ideas about salvation?

Fifth, righteousness is given by union with Christ. Believers "become the righteousness of God in Him" (2 Cor. 5:21). Notice that it is "in Christ" that we become the righteousness of God. It is union with Christ that gives it. We are either in Adam or in Christ; in

Adam there is condemnation and death, but in Christ there is righteousness and life (1 Cor. 15:22). Have you accepted that there are two representative heads to humanity, Adam and Christ? Have you recognized that righteousness can be had only by being removed from Adam and placed into Christ? Often people object to the idea of Christ's active obedience being imputed because they don't understand their true state of condemnation in Adam (Rom. 5:12–21).

Sixth, Christ is our righteousness. "You are in Christ Jesus, who became for us wisdom from God—and righteousness and sanctification and redemption" (1 Cor. 1:30). We see here that Christ is given to us for certain purposes: to provide us wisdom, redemption, and sanctification but also to provide us righteousness. Clearly, then, Christ's righteousness was not only for the purpose of making Him an acceptable sacrifice, though it mercifully did that too. The righteousness we get by being united with Him when we believe the gospel is His.

John Bunyan suffered around two years of misery and doubt after he made a profession of faith in Christ. He would sometimes wander the countryside feeling as if God was going to damn his soul despite his feeble attempts to believe. He struggled because he kept looking at himself—his weak performance and unruly and frightening thoughts. The end result was that he had almost no assurance of salvation. One day, after much agony and prayer and Bible study, a thought came to him while he was walking. "Your righteousness is in heaven." He rushed home to find this statement in the Bible, to be sure that he wasn't just following his own thoughts. At first, he began to despair because he couldn't find the statement, but after a while he discovered 1 Corinthians 1:30 and realized that the idea, though not the exact clause, was there. He rejoiced because he realized that Christ made up for all his lack.[4] Bunyan had found a gospel worth preaching, and he became one of the greatest preachers of his era.

Seventh, Christ's righteousness is imputed to His people. David spoke of "the blessedness of the man to whom God imputes

---

4. This story is related in Bunyan's autobiography, *Grace Abounding to the Chief of Sinners.*

righteousness apart from works" (Rom. 4:6). Here we see that righteousness is indeed imputed to believers, and given the texts we've already examined, this righteousness is Jesus Christ's and is given by virtue of union with Him.[5] This teaching fits with Old Testament expectations, where we are told that the Lord would be "our righteousness" (Jer. 23:6) and that the Messiah would bring in "everlasting righteousness" (Dan. 9:24).

In summation, Christ's active obedience means that He perfectly obeyed the law and imputed His perfect obedience to the believer's account in God's sight. It really is true—believers are as righteous as Jesus Christ in God's sight. That is shocking, but it is clearly the teaching of Scripture. In Christ we are made the righteousness of God (2 Cor. 5:21).

This teaching enriches the picture of God's love and our sin. Terms like *grace* can become trite, but when we flesh out doctrines

---

5. Some have misunderstood Romans 4:5 ("faith is accounted for righteousness") to mean that faith *is* our righteousness. This mistaken interpretation denies that Christ's righteousness is imputed to the believer. The problems with this view are many: first, the word *for* in Romans 4:5 and other verses like it is the Greek word εἰς, which most often refers to movement toward a goal. Rather than faith *being* a believer's righteousness, it *leads one to* a righteous condition—in Christ. Therefore, a correct translation would be "faith is accounted unto righteousness." Second, Paul's language elsewhere is clear about faith leading us to a righteous condition, not its being our righteousness. "With the heart one believes unto righteousness" (Rom. 10:10). In other words, when a person by God's grace believes the gospel, he becomes righteous. Other Scripture makes it clear that God unites the believer with Christ, and by virtue of that union the believer is declared righteous because Christ is righteous. The believer's faith led him "unto" that righteous condition. Third, denying the imputation of Christ's righteousness ignores the many Scriptures that teach that Christ is our righteousness (1 Cor. 1:30) and that we gain righteousness by being united to Him (2 Cor. 5:21). Faith is the instrument of our being declared righteous, while Christ is the basis of our being declared righteous. It is as if someone were to ask, "On what basis should this sinner be considered righteous?" The correct answer is, "He has believed the gospel, and therefore Christ's merit is his own." A popular hymn says, "No merit of my own, his anger to suppress, my only hope is Jesus's blood and righteousness." The key thing to remember, in the simplest terms, is that biblical faith rests on Jesus, not itself. The hymn does not say "my only hope is my own hope." Faith is not our righteousness before God; Christ is. Faith, when it is biblical faith, latches on to Christ, not itself (Heb. 6:19–20).

like Christ's active obedience, we begin to appreciate the idea once more. When I understand that Christ's righteousness is imputed to me, it becomes apparent that my problem as a sinner is not merely that I was under condemnation for my sin, a curse that Christ graciously endured in my place on the cross. I also had no active righteousness. It wasn't just that I had a punishment I could not endure; I had a debt I could not pay. Christ died to endure God's punishment for me, and He obeyed to impute His obedience to me. He paid the penalty and provides the positive wealth. In so many ways, Christ meets all my profound spiritual needs.

Most to the point, this teaching helps remove fear of the last judgment, which usually revolves around sins we've committed or things we should have done but failed to do. We fear judgment because we feel as though our life is draped in filthy rags of sin, so standing before God is a terrifying thought. Our sins are like an army surrounding us, as John Flavel so eloquently put it. In the afterlife, our sins will all rise and follow us to judgment, crying out, "We are thy sins, and we will follow thee."[6] But in Christ our debt is paid, our sins wiped out, and even more, His works are our own. If you believe in Christ, there will be no horde of sins crying you down and accusing you. There will also be no silence when a godly testimony must be heard about you. The filthy, shameful rags are gone and replaced by Christ's perfect robe of righteousness. The howling crowd of accusers is gone, replaced by the pure voices of testimony. O the joy! And what's more, does this news not motivate you to love and serve the one who has provided so for you, even when you were unaware of it and could not appreciate it?

Christ Suffered the Curse for Me

We have focused on Christ's active obedience, which to some Christians is a lost or absent doctrine. Here we concentrate on the more commonly known passive obedience: "Christ has redeemed us from the curse of the law, having become a curse for us" (Gal. 3:13).

---

6. Flavel, *Fountain of Life*, 139.

The curse Paul refers to is death, which God metes out to people who break His law. There are "wages" to sin, we are told (Rom. 6:23), which is a fascinating metaphor. We are familiar with the idea of agreeing with an employer about an hourly wage based on fulfilling a condition—the "job." Most of us live in such arrangements constantly. Romans 6:23 tells us that all people are in an analogous arrangement with God, but rather than being given a job and a monetary wage, the wage is death for those who commit sin. And since we have all sinned (3:23), we all get the wage.

This arrangement is stringent—the wage is earned by even one sinful act. "Cursed is everyone who does not continue in all things which are written in the book of the law, to do them" (Gal. 3:10). God demands perfect obedience, or else He metes out death—spiritual death (Eph. 2:1–3), physical death (Gen. 5:5–31), and eternal death (Rev. 21:8). That's a strict arrangement.

The arrangement is widespread—the curse of the law is on us because of Adam's sin. He disobeyed and brought death into the world (Rom. 5:12, 17; Gen. 2:17). But his sin did not merely set a negative example that we all unfortunately followed. He represented his descendants, and his covenant was their covenant. When he disobeyed, his sin "made" us guilty sinners (Rom. 5:19). Because of union with Adam, people suffer the curse of death: "In Adam all die" (1 Cor. 15:22).

But it is important to note that we are not absolved of guilt, as if it were Adam who got us into this mess, not us. In federal relationships it is easy to shift blame on the leaders. We're guilty in Adam, but we've also personally sinned more times than we can count. Our sins make our situation even more serious. They store up wrath, or heap it up (Rom. 2:5; James 5:3).

The result of all this is that people in Adam are eternally separated from God at death. God is holy and will never allow anything sinful to dwell with Him. "You are not a God who takes pleasure in wickedness, nor shall evil dwell with You" (Ps. 5:4). "There shall by no means enter it [heaven] anything that defiles, or causes an abomination or a lie" (Rev. 21:27). Instead of being with God, they will enter "everlasting fire prepared for the devil and his angels" (Matt. 25:41).

When Christ died on the cross, He paid our wage. He suffered our curse. He died in our place and appeased the wrath of God against us. One result is reconciliation with God: "We were reconciled to God through the death of His Son" (Rom. 5:10). Another result is salvation from God's just wrath: "We shall be saved from wrath through Him" (v. 9). The wrath of God, the curse for sin, the broken covenant of works, and all of our heaped up sin can no longer harm us. God punished Christ on the cross for our sins (Isa. 53:6). God would be unjust to punish the same sins twice. If you are a repentant believer in Christ, your sins are gone, and you really are saved, for Christ's perfect work abolished the record of debt that God held against you (Col. 2:14). You failed at the job and earned the wage of death; the list of your wrongs was long and recorded in the omniscient mind of God. But Christ paid the wage and wiped out the list.

Let this news quiet your conscience. God smiles on you in Christ and always will. Let this mighty truth allay any servile fears about the judgment and instill joy in you. If death is the punishment for sin, and the definition of death includes eternal damnation, then Christ has freed us from eternal damnation, and the assurances of John 3:16 are true: whoever believes in Christ will not perish but have everlasting life.

Christ Ever Lives to Intercede for Me

Christ's saving ministry didn't end at the cross or at the resurrection. He continues His ministry as high priest. When He ascended, He sat down at the Father's right hand (Col. 3:1; Heb. 1:3). He is also said to stand in the midst of the Father's throne (Rev. 5:6) and to have taken a seat on His Father's throne (3:21). He stood when Stephen was martyred (Acts 7:56). The variation of imagery isn't meant to confuse us but rather to show us what is really important—Christ ministers in God's presence as high priest: "We have a great High Priest who has passed through the heavens, Jesus the Son of God" (Heb. 4:14). His sitting communicates His prerogative (1:13) as well as the completeness of His work on the cross (Heb. 10:11–14). His standing may point to the activity and efficacy of His work or the keen interest Christ has in carrying it out. His standing at Stephen's death may say something poignant about His attitude toward His people's suffering. When Stephen, His faithful witness, was cruelly martyred, Christ rose to His feet.

A primary thing that Christ is presently doing in His high priestly ministry is interceding for His people (Rom. 8:34). Intercession means to entreat someone, such as an authority, on behalf of someone else. The high priest in the Old Testament took the blood from the altar and brought it into the temple to make atonement for the people; it is said of Christ, "With His own blood He entered the Most Holy Place once for all" (Heb. 9:12). Not that Christ brought literal blood into heaven; His blood was like the key unlocking heaven so He could enter it as our forerunner. His acceptance there, where evil cannot come, is the ultimate proof of the perfection of His sacrifice. His dwelling at God's right hand eternally declares that He has propitiated God's wrath against elect sinners. Christ's presence exudes sweet peace in heaven like a fragrance. He is "sweet peace enthroned with smiles."[7] The best way to understand His intercession is to see it as essentially "the virtual continuation of his offering once made on earth."[8]

Consider the meaning of having an "Advocate with the Father" (1 John 2:1). At God's right hand, a crucified, resurrected Son of David ever sits as high priest. No prosecutor can accuse believers or make any claim stick (see Rev. 12:10), for Christ has an irrefutable defense— He paid their wage and endured their curse. They are safe as long as Christ lives, and He lives forever. "He is…able to save to the uttermost those who come to God through Him, since He always lives to make intercession for them" (Heb. 7:25). The words "save to the uttermost" are striking—His endless life ensures believers' endless salvation. There is also something precious in the words "He always lives to make intercession," as if the whole purpose of His endless life is to care for and protect His people. In fact, that is exactly what the

7. Henry Vaughan, "Peace," in *The Complete Poems* (New Haven, Conn.: Yale University Press, 1976), 185–86.
8. Flavel, *Fountain of Life*, 151.

words mean. He has so bound Himself to His people that His continued life is all about their safety and eternal blessedness.

Christ Will Uphold His Advocacy for Me at the Judgment

This truth is a necessary consequence to all we have said thus far. It is unthinkable that Christ would come into the world to save His people, live for them, die for them, be resurrected to intercede for them forever, only to lose them at the judgment. He Himself denied this would ever happen. "I give them eternal life, and they shall never perish" (John 10:28). The word *perish* is the same word used in John 3:16: "Whoever believes in Him should not perish but have everlasting life." Perishing is the opposite of eternal life and therefore refers to eternal death. It refers to the destruction of "both soul and body in hell" (Matt. 10:28), where there is eternal torment (Luke 16:28; Rev. 14:11). This horror is what Jesus promises will never happen to believers: "He who believes in the Son has everlasting life" (John 3:36). Flavel said that Christ "died to save them, and he will never…overthrow the designs and ends of his own death."[9]

God emphasizes that His forgiveness is complete and permanent now and forever. He has taken our sins as far away as possible: "As far as the east is from the west" (Ps. 103:12). He permanently disposed of our sin: "You will cast all our sins into the depths of the sea" (Mic. 7:19). God permanently forgets their sin: "Their sin I will remember no more" (Jer. 31:34). God cannot forget anything, yet He promises to deal with believers as if He can completely and permanently do so. This complete salvation exists only due to Christ's redemptive work: "You are complete in Him" (Col. 2:10). With Christ as our advocate, the last judgment is clearly something to be anticipated with joy.

God will not only uphold our forgiven status at the judgment but will also reward all our efforts to serve Him. There is hardly anything more remarkable than this, for we deserve eternal punishment. God is monumentally gracious to give Christ, forgive sins,

---

9. Flavel, *Fountain of Life*, 525.

and deliver from wrath. But in a move of more staggering graciousness, He rewards our service, even though all the glory for it is due to Him, for our fruit is from Him (1 Cor. 15:10; Hos. 14:8). He even calls it injustice not to reward us: "God is not unjust to forget your work and labor of love" (Heb. 6:10). That is so kind that it should make us absolutely humbled yet jubilant in our gracious God. As we saw earlier, God rewards the smallest efforts, like a cup of cold water given in His name. He even accepts Christians' imperfect and bungling service, because Christ, their perfect high priest, sanctifies all their efforts (Ex. 28:36–38; 1 Peter 2:5). John Calvin wrote that "in Christ he sets a value on our works, which in themselves deserve nothing."[10] The last judgment is not something to dread; believers will rejoice and be staggered at the gracious kindness of God.

Dark Clouds of Wrath, Shining Door of Gospel

It may be that you have been influenced by careless things people say about the judgment. Perhaps it was presented to you as a time when all your sins would become public and you would be shamed. (The unspoken inference was, "So you'd better be good!") Perhaps it was presented as a time when all your sins would be ferreted out, your "dirty laundry" put on display, your sins weighed in the balance, and a decision made as to whether you are good enough, all while you stand in dread and nail-biting uncertainty.

People who speak this way aren't necessarily trying to be oppressive; they probably just want to keep people from sinning and are falling into overly controlling means, perhaps out of fear. It is admittedly important to warn sinners of the dark clouds of coming wrath, but simultaneously the shining door of the gospel should always be opened to them. It is right to instill godly fear in people but not a dread that is devoid of faith in a gracious God (see Luke 12:5, 7). Attempts at controlling behavior through fear can be haunting in a very negative way, and the overall effect makes people unsettled in their thoughts about Christianity, which is supposed to provide

---

10. Calvin, *1 John*, 2:66.

believers a basis for eternal joy, not dread. Somehow people can become confused and use religious thoughts as tools to control, and even oppress, rather than to present the glorious gospel to sinners who need conviction to lead them to hope in Christ. My prayer is that this presentation of the judgment of believers will inspire joy and instill longing for Christ in the hearts of repentant believers.

The best way to motivate people to serve Christ and avoid evil is to display Christ's love. This forgotten hymn by John Newton gets the idea across better than nearly anything I know:

> Lord, Thou hast won, at length I yield,
> My heart, by mighty grace compelled,
> Surrenders all to Thee;
> Against Thy terrors long I strove,
> But who can stand against Thy love?
> Love conquers even me.
>
> If thou hadst bid thy thunders roll
> Or lightnings flash to blast my soul,
> I still had stubborn been;
> But mercy hath my heart subdued
> A bleeding savior I have viewed
> And now I hate my sin.[11]

11. John Newton, "The Rebel's Surrender to Grace," in *Olney Hymns*, 121, stanzas 1 and 4.

Study Questions

1. Will Christians "get a pass" at judgment? Will they not be judged according to their works?

2. In what way will the judgment of Christians be different from the judgment of unbelievers?

3. What Scriptures make clear that the judgment of Christians will be different from that of unbelievers?

4. If you are a repentant believer in Christ, have you welcomed the biblical picture of what judgment will be like for you? Or do you think of judgment as a fearful thing that may result in your eternal doom?

5. How do we know there will be no negative surprises after death for believers?

6. Some people will discover that theirs will be the judgment of an unbeliever (Matt. 7:21–23). With truths like this in Scripture, how can you avoid a life of dread and uncertainty?

7. Explain how Christ is our basis for anticipating the judgment with joy.

8. What does it mean that "Christ obeyed for me"?

9. What does it mean that "Christ suffered the curse for me?"

10. What does it mean that "Christ ever lives to intercede for me"?

11. How do we know that Christ will uphold His advocacy of believers at the last judgment?

12. Have you rested in all that Christ is for a Christian? Could it be that you have failed to experience joy because you haven't?

13. Why might Christians sometimes present judgment only and not grace?

Our Joy and God's Glory

A whole book on seeking joy may seem to encourage a self-centered approach to the Christian life. Nevertheless, the fact remains that we are commanded to rejoice in Christ (Phil. 4:4; 1 Thess. 5:16). Joy is an essential emotional response to the gospel, and when it wanes in our lives we slight God's grace. Of course, seeking happiness outside of Christ is idolatrous. But seeking joy in Christ means seeking to live, think, and feel as a consistent Christian. God has devised a way of salvation that makes it right and necessary to endlessly rejoice. He has inextricably linked our joy and His glory. "Whoever offers praise glorifies Me" (Ps. 50:23). To quote Charles Bridges, "Lie not against the truth by allowing your countenance to display gloom."[1]

Therefore, it is not self-centered to seek joy in Christ; it is necessary if we are to fulfill the chief end of man. To seek biblical joy is to have a passion for God's glory and to seek the honor due to His name in our very souls. So, we must get busy being happy in Jesus and assist others in doing the same. It is remarkable, isn't it? God wants us to be happy, and He isn't satisfied unless we are.

Here is one Scripture where many of the threads appear: "Let all those who seek You rejoice and be glad in You; and let those who love Your salvation say continually, 'Let God be magnified!'" (Ps. 70:4). You can see that all believers should rejoice, not just some of them; that they should do so out of love for God's salvation; that joy is connected to the glory of God; and that our joy should effusively praise God continually.

---

1. Adapted from Bridges, *Proverbs*, 274.

The acid test of whether our faith has really influenced us is whether it has produced joy in us. We are made happy by what we value and see as truly beneficial. If theology doesn't make us happy, then we must conclude that we don't believe it or value it. To put it simply, we don't like it. Since theology is simply thoughts about God, we must conclude we don't like thinking of Him; to bring it down to "brass tacks," it means we don't like Him. The Christian community should be a passionate place of knowing God as He has revealed Himself in the Word, of rejoicing in that knowledge, and of shining the light of it in our own heart and each other's (see Mal. 3:16).

It is true that even seeking joy "in Christ" can become selfish when it is divorced from reverence for God and obedience to His Word. This point deserves restating, for I suspect that nothing is more common in our times than the lawless seeking of pleasure under a religious banner. This is worldliness—but with the unfortunate addition of religious hypocrisy. "Joy in Christ" without obedience to His commands does not glorify God; it insults Him, for it seeks Him as savior but rejects Him as lord. "Why do you call me 'Lord, Lord,' and not do the things which I say?" (Luke 6:46). If you find yourself in the terrible place of antinomianism, humbly flee to Christ in repentant faith, seeking cleansing by His blood. Ask for His Spirit to empower you to obey. Believe that He doesn't cast you away, and go forward on your knees seeking to live and think and feel according to His commandments.

A book like this is unlikely to please everyone. Some people might feel that I belabored things and others might feel that I shortchanged other things. I could have labored over this book for many years. The chapters could be lengthened and further chapters added, all in an attempt to be as comprehensive as possible. There could have been chapters such as "Joy in the Mundane" or "Joy When You Are Under Pressure" or "Joy When You Are Isolated." Those would be worthy entries, as might many others. (I invite you to flesh out how to have biblical joy in those dark places yourself.) The fact that there are so many potential topics shows the relevance of the theme of joy and the veritable army of things that challenge it. The need of a book like this is very apparent, as is the need of our continual efforts to extract joy from God's Word as we continue our pilgrimage through this vale of tears.

But rather than compose a lengthy, comprehensive tome, I decided to write something more accessible that attempts to instill an impulse—to shine the light of God's truth in dark places so that you can rejoice despite living in this vale of tears. This idea is fleshed out sufficiently to give a glimpse of something much bigger—a theology that leads to joy. Thoughts about God must lead to peace, joy, prayer, gratitude, and obedience, no matter the circumstance.

The impulse to rejoice can and ought to be practiced whether faced with dark things or blessings. Whenever you experience a hardship of any sort, ask, "What truth about God ministers joy in this particular dark place?" When you are reading a passage of Scripture that speaks of something dark, ask, "How do the promises of the gospel minister joy despite these unsettling matters?" When you are studying biblical doctrine, ask, "Why should this theological truth inspire joy in me?" When you find a promise in the Word, ask, "How can I shine this light on my particular hardship?" When you are made happy by circumstances, tell yourself, "This earthly blessing is a symbol of spiritual blessings and a small beam in the sun of mercy."

There's always the danger of focusing so much on an important character trait, in this case joy, that the basis for it gets obscured. We must not replace Christ with joy or move the gaze of the soul from Him to the subject of rejoicing in Him. To rejoice in Him properly, we must constantly fix our eyes on Him, not on joy, and it is that instinct that I have tried to instill in this book. I have tried to discuss the subject of rejoicing in Christ all the while gazing at Christ. I desperately hope I've succeeded, for there is a terrible tendency in our hearts to obsess about self or make religion all about therapy.

But despite the danger of navel-gazing, we do have the capacity of self-reflection, and there is nothing wrong with being sure that our subjective response to God's objective truth is godly. We must do so. A significant amount of attention must be given to ourselves, just as Paul told Timothy: "Take heed to yourself and to the doctrine" (1 Tim. 4:16). Giving attention to ourselves, our subjective responses to God and to the world, is not ipso facto self-centered navel-gazing. We must be sure to rejoice in order to glorify God.

It must be said that we need God's grace to have joy in dark places. Thankfully, in the gospel, we have the empowerment of the Spirit. God-given truth about Christ, residing in the soul of a person who is filled with the Spirit, is powerful. It strengthens the soul in a subtle but profound way. This internal ballast is what Paul referred to when he stated, "Be strong in the grace that is in Christ Jesus" (2 Tim. 2:1). We need this internal, joyous strength because in this sin-cursed world, there will always be a cold blast of trouble, a shadow of hardship. But with God's truth kindled in the soul by the Spirit, we will have plenty of spiritual light and warmth.

Ultimately I wrote this book because I personally have to wrestle with the reality of Philippians 4:4: "Rejoice in the Lord always." In a very real way, my Christian life has been (and still is) one long rec-onciliation with the truth of that verse and others like it. Christianity must produce joy. Its news is too revolutionary and forcible to leave a person uninspired and grumbling, no matter the family issues, health problems, societal decay, or the vacuous church's sad state of corrup-tion. I must rejoice in the Lord, by God's grace, even if the worst comes to pass (Hab. 3:17–18). My bent to be a miserable curmudgeon must be combated by the Word and the Spirit at every turn (Ps. 119:11; Gal. 5:16; Rom. 8:13). This book is the result of my doing so, and I pray I continue to do so, for every day presents new challenges.

The basic rationale of this book is crystal clear in Isaiah, a ratio-nale we all must live every moment of our lives: "My soul shall be joyful in my God; for He has clothed me with the garments of salva-tion, He has covered me with the robe of righteousness" (Isa. 61:10). In short, God's salvation has a logic to it, demanding that we respond to it with abundant joy, and if we don't have joy at any given moment, at that moment we are failing to grasp the gospel's great-ness. Yes, there will be times when other fitting emotions should take precedence in our hearts. But that doesn't change the normative role of joy in the believer's life. Our Christian lives must be a continual Spirit-empowered effort to stay in tune with the gospel so that we rejoice in God and glorify Him. My prayer is that all your thoughts of God might lead to the praise of Christ, to empowerment by His Spirit, and to biblical joy.